Inspiration Points

Where Our Writers Wrote

Clark Beim-Esche

Published by FastPencil Publishing

Inspiration Points

First Edition

Copyright © Clark Beim-Esche 2020

All rights reserved. No part of this publication may be reproduced, stored in a retrieval system, or transmitted, in any form, or by any means, electronic, mechanical, photocopying, recording, or otherwise, without the prior consent of the publisher.

Sale of this book without a front cover may be unauthorized. If the book is coverless, it may have been reported to the publisher as "unsold or destroyed" and neither the author nor the publisher may have received payment for it.

Although every precaution has been taken to verify the accuracy of the information contained herein, the author and publisher assume no responsibility for any errors or omissions. No liability is assumed for damages that may result from the use of information contained within.

http://www.fastpencil.com

Printed in the United States of America

Table of Contents

Why This Book Came to Be ix
Preface xii
Washington Irving 15
Henry Wadsworth Longfellow 29
Ralph Waldo Emerson 47
Henry David Thoreau 61
Bronson and Louisa May Alcott 83
Nathaniel Hawthorne 97
Emily Dickinson 115
Harriet Beecher Stowe 129
Mark Twain 149
Ernest Hemingway 207
Margaret Mitchell 219
Robert Frost 237
Locations Visited 253
A Select Bibliography 259
Afterword 265
About the Author 269

Once again, I dedicate a book to my wife, Carol. Without her love, her tireless labor, and her perceptive thought, neither our travels nor this book would have been possible.

Why This Book Came to Be

Most, if not all, of the twelve writers who are the subject of this book, are familiar names. Many of them enjoyed wide popular success during their lifetimes. Many have been at one time or another universally praised and considered to be of major literary and/or historical significance. Which begs the question, "Why write yet another appreciation of authors whose works have already come to hold prominent positions in the history of American literature?"

My answer is simple. Because my wife, Carol, and I have traveled to the homes and settings in which these authors wrote, and doing so has been a revelation. It has given us fresh insights into the lives, works, and creative processes of these twelve well-known, yet still tantalizingly challenging, writers.

And sometimes, even more gratifyingly, these places themselves have provided unexpected information that has moderated, even occasionally negated, criticisms levied at the work of each of these writers.

Standing in the tiny vestibule in Longfellow's childhood home in Portland, Maine, where young Henry fled for refuge from his many brothers and sisters in order to practice his poetic craft in peace, one can't help but sympathize with the monumental task he had set out for himself.

Looking out the upstairs study window of Emerson's The Old Manse near Concord, one sees the site of the Old North Bridge and the battlefield where the British retreat to Boston had begun in April of 1775. What clarity this setting adds to the opening sentence of his great work, *Nature* which he wrote in that very room: "Our age is retrospective. It builds the sepulchers of the fathers."

I have strolled through the graveyard of King's Chapel in downtown Boston where a youthful Nathaniel Hawthorne used to take his lunch hour when he was employed in the nearby Custom House. Imagine my feeling when, while reading some of the headstones that he would have seen many times, I happened on the early 18th century grave marker of Elizabeth Pain with its half-concealed letter "A."

The meadow behind Robert Frost's farm in Derry, New Hampshire, still sends out its quiet invitation, "You come too." And on the edge of the property the rocky "Mending Wall" continues to invite each visitor to contemplate both the worth and the cost of such "good fences."

When Carol and I stood in the living room of "The Dump," the small apartment in downtown Atlanta where Margaret Mitchell crafted her masterpiece, *Gone with the Wind*, any claim of romanticism simply melted away. Her intent in writing, it became evident, was in no way a celebration of the "beauty" of the "Lost Cause" of the Confederacy.

These places, and many others, have been most illuminating experiences for Carol and me. These writers' "Inspiration Points" have led us to discover titles we had never read and also to return to familiar books with renewed interest and energy. Carol and I invite you to travel along with us as we expand and deepen our understanding of what these authors achieved. We hope that you will agree with us that it is a journey well worth taking.

> <u>Front Cover</u>: *Mark Twain's Octagonal Study relocated to the campus of Elmira College, Elmira, NY*
> <u>Back Cover</u>: *Henry David Thoreau's One Room Cabin (replica) near Walden Pond in Concord, MA*

Preface

Here might be a good place to begin, I told myself. Here in this quiet hillside section of Sleepy Hollow cemetery near the town of Concord, Massachusetts. After all, this was some of American literature's holiest ground, the final resting place of four of our greatest writers. And here too was memorialized one of our country's most noteworthy philosophic movements.

During the early half of the 19th century and continuing for several decades thereafter, Concord had been the epicenter of America's first great golden age of thought and literature. Here, Transcendentalism had taken root. Here, a New World Romanticism had flourished which would, in later years, mellow into a grounded and humane Realism. And the words and ideas of these revered authors still resonate in this place. Of course, their audible voices are silent now, but both their writings and the nearby locales and homes where they lived and labored continue to cast clarifying and inspirational light on their achievements, providing a perspective very different from what is typically mentioned in school texts or history books.

As a college and college-prep English teacher for over thirty years, I have been saddened when I have occasionally heard disinterested dismissals of America's so-called "canonical writers" of the 19th and early 20th centuries. Naysayers insist that these "dead white men," however venerated they may have been in their own times, come across today as unattached to, and unmindful of, the needs and concerns of contemporary readers.

In fact, nothing could be further from the truth.

First, these authors were not all men. Second, they were acutely sensitive to and conscious of the fact that they were forging new intellectual landscapes with their writings and expressed thoughts. Most important, they were vitally interested in discovering and wrestling with questions growing directly out of their experiences as Americans, questions that today's men and women continue to find both challenging and dauntingly essential. How can a person define and measure success in life? Is it possible to escape the consequences of one's past? Is a new beginning truly a fresh start? To what extent are we irrevocably defined by race or gender? Is it too late to be a seeker—and, more importantly, a finder—of Truth? Such questions form the core of the writings of these remarkable men and women.

And the homes and the settings of the literature they produced create vivid backdrops for the inspired insights and memorably eloquent answers they set forth in the books they have left us.

On this late November day in 2015, my wife, Carol, and I slowly made our way up a steep hillside on a rather roughly paved walkway in order to pay our respects. Once we arrived at the top, there on the right, beneath a humble stone marker no more than ten inches high and bearing only the name "Henry," lay the mortal remains of Henry David Thoreau, the prose poet of Walden Pond. On the opposite side of the path, and set apart by a chained off border, the gravestones of Nathaniel Hawthorne and his beloved wife, Sophia, were visible. Farther up on the right and clustered near the walkway, the headstones of Bronson Alcott, his long-suffering wife, Abigail, and stone markers for their daughters Beth, May, and Louisa May, cast delicate shadows over the path's edge and the tangle of interlaced roots visible among the pine needles which covered the ground around them. Past the crest of the hill and a bit to the right, a jagged piece of striated granite jutted up, the monument of the Sage of Concord, Ralph Waldo Emerson. His grave was flanked by the stones of two women who had shared their lives with him: Lidian Jackson, the wife of his maturity and mother of his children, and Ellen Tucker Emerson, their firstborn daughter, loving caregiver during her father's last years and namesake of the wife of his youth. Emerson's stone included a plaque containing a brief verse, descriptive both of his character and of the expansive and vital Truth to which he had devoted his life's work:

The Passive Master lent his hand
To the Vast Soul that o'er him planned.

The autumn day was unseasonably fine, its temperature near 60 degrees, with thin white clouds scudding across a pale blue sky. A persistent wind rushed through the grove of pine trees whose lowest limbs were still twenty or thirty feet above our heads. We took another quiet look around the hillside, and then carefully began retracing our steps back down the steep walkway toward our waiting car. Yes, I reassured myself, America's early writers deserve to be remembered and valued.

Of course, Carol and I would have many miles to travel in order to see the homes of all the authors about whom I wanted to write. But, this visit had been a perfect "Inspiration Point" for us before commencing. Time now to begin our journeys.

1

Washington Irving

My Unscheduled Stop

Washington Irving's Sunnyside in Irvington, New York

There are two stories regarding Washington Irving that I particularly enjoy sharing with my friends. One is a personal remembrance resulting from one of my many travels within the United States. The other is a tale that was told to us by a docent at Irving's New York home "Sunnyside" located on the eastern banks of the Hudson River near the Tappan Zee. The first story illustrates the surprising magnitude of his literary productivity. The second reveals the considerable extent of the love and respect his reputation had earned for him by the closing years of his life.

Bust of Washington Irving

My first story dates back to the summer of 2009 when Carol and I were traveling to several presidential sites in Ohio gathering materials for my book *Calling on the Presidents: Tales Their Houses Tell*. We had begun our swing around Ohio in its northwest quarter visiting Spiegel Grove in Fremont, the home of Rutherford Hayes, our 19th President. The site's spacious grounds were breathtaking and the forest of trees planted there, an inspiration. The home itself was meticulously kept, and our tour was led by an enthusiastic and knowledgeable docent.

My favorite room in the house, as was somewhat typical of me, was the president's private study. The walls were lined with books as well as with images of President Hayes' military friends and comrades-in-arms. Just as our guide was leading us out of this room in order to tour other areas of the house, my eye was caught by a line of books arrayed on a shelf near the door through which we were about to exit. It was a red cloth set, each volume of which carried the simple label "Irving's Works." But what had arrested me had not been the relatively ordinary binding of these books. It was their number that had impressed me. "One, two, three," I began counting, "seven, eight, nine," then "sixteen, seventeen, eighteen," and finally "twenty-five, twenty-six, twenty-seven."

Twenty-seven volumes of works written by Washington Irving!? I knew of only two stories penned by this writer: "Rip Van Winkle" and "The Legend of Sleepy Hollow." Two questions arose immediately in my mind. First, what else, in heaven's name, could be contained in this expansive collection? And, second, why would a prestigious New York publisher like G. P. Putnam's Sons risk printing such a large number of volumes written by this frequently overlooked writer?

I had the answer to my second question almost before I had finished asking it of myself. Established publishers *don't* take risks, particularly when producing sets of an author's complete works. Those twenty-seven volumes were telling me that I had underestimated just how important and well-known Washington Irving had been to his immediate audience.

My first question, of course, could only be answered in one way. So as soon as we returned home to St. Louis, I went to the internet site of my favorite bookseller, found a listing for a twenty-seven-volume set of "Irving's Works," and ordered it.

The books arrived in a couple of weeks, and I did note that the final three volumes were a "Life and Letters" biography of Irving written by his nephew, Pierre. Nevertheless there remained twenty-four volumes all written by Washington Irving, a robust reading project that would come to spread out over several years. But I was determined to keep at it. If I, and to be fair, if the teachers who had been in charge of my education, had given Washington Irving an undeservedly short shrift, I wanted to discover what I had missed. And the answer to that question, as it turned out, put simply was "A great deal indeed." Thus began my gradual and prolonged delve into the collected works of Washington Irving.

Some brief biographical research revealed that, despite the ultimate girth of Irving's literary output, his family's original plan for this, their youngest son, was more down to earth. They had wanted Washington to position himself in an occupation that would ensure his prosperity and financial security. They encouraged him to study law. In 1801, he dutifully began clerking at some prestigious law firms, but he also started to write satirical articles on issues of the day. Perhaps to protect his professional career, he wrote under a pseudonym, but he clearly enjoyed the positive response his pieces began to receive. By 1804, however, his health had begun to decline, and his family arranged a trip for him to England and the European continent. This respite, they hoped, would both give him a chance to recuperate and allow him to meet and experience new people and places. He could take the New York bar exam after this holiday, they reasoned. And upon his return home in 1806, he did so, narrowly passing the bar, after which he began to establish his legal practice.

Yet even while pursuing this career, Irving continued to write. In 1809 he published his first book. Still using a pseudonym, Diedrich Knickerbocker, Irving produced the volume which began my chronologically arranged reading program: *A History of New York from the Beginning of the World to the End of the Dutch Dynasty*

(1809). As even its extended title suggests, this work, rather than being simply another dry historical chronicle, was a witty and often hilarious satire of the period of the history of Manhattan in the years preceding the British takeover of the city. But the fact that it was also written by a native New Yorker, both sharpened and lovingly softened its tone. He concluded his cleverly constructed "history" with the following assurance to his readers:

> *I am none of those cynics who despise the world, because it despises them: on the contrary, though but low in its regard, I look up to it with the most perfect good-nature, and my only sorrow is, that it does not prove itself more worthy of the unbounded love I bear it. (524)*

This passage, I have come to believe, epitomizes the unique quality of the writing style of Washington Irving. He possessed an almost uncanny ability to both critically analyze and simultaneously admire the world about which he was writing. A world that, as I continued to read, was constantly widening its borders.

Even though his *History of New York* enjoyed a gratifying success, Irving would not write another book for over ten years. By 1815 he found himself traveling back to England on important family business. His brother Peter was running the European operations of P. and E. Irving, a trading concern which had been struggling since the War of 1812. Washington, it was hoped, might be able to help him turn things around and increase the operation's financial standing. But despite his efforts to salvage the enterprise, Irving was unable to avert the company's ultimate bankruptcy.

This left the young man professionally adrift for the time being, but he quickly returned to the vocation that had always commanded his greatest interest: literature.

During the seventeen years he would spend in Europe (1815-1832), he produced seven books, works that ultimately made him a literary celebrity. The opening sentence of his first effort (and the second book on my reading list), *The Sketch Book of Geoffrey Crayon, Gent* (1819-20), stated what would become Irving's central theme: "I was always fond of visiting new scenes, and observing strange characters and manners." In fact, it was this fondness for "visiting new scenes" that would come to define almost the entirety of his remarkable literary life and work.

The Sketch Book (1819-20), *Bracebridge Hall* (1822), and *Tales of a Traveller* (1824) all attested to Irving's indefatigable interest in visiting new places throughout both England and continental Europe, meeting interesting people, and recounting the many stories they had to tell. He then moved into historical narratives with *History of the Life and Voyages of Christopher Columbus* (1828), *Chronicle of the Conquest of Granada* (1829), *Voyages and Discoveries of the Companions of Columbus* (1831), and finally *Tales of the Alhambra* (1832) in which he combined historical accounts with fascinating tales associated with that storied locale in which he had been able to reside for two years. Throughout all these works, Irving consistently described new "scenes" and "characters" with a spirit of enthusiastic appreciation. In later years, while remembering his extended visit to the home of Sir Walter Scott, Irving wrote a sentence that best expressed his entire way of living and seeing: "Every night I retired with my mind filled with delightful recollections of the day, and every morning I rose with the certainty of new enjoyment" ("Abbotsford" in *Crayon Miscellany* 326). This combination of gratitude for past opportunities and an unshakable expectation of future joys formed the very essence of his character.

And it is to the private study of Rutherford B. Hayes that I am indebted for helping me discover the many works and unique spirit of this remarkable man, the first American author to achieve wide acclaim in Europe, and the first American to be able to support himself solely through his writing. Sometimes such unintended consequences can enrich our lives in ways we never could have imagined.

My second favorite story regarding Washington Irving was related to me during the summer of the very next year, 2010.

Once again, Carol and I had been traveling with the purpose of collecting information for my book regarding the homes of our past presidents. This time we had journeyed further east to visit some of the residences of the Chief Executives who had lived in the state of New York. We crossed the Hudson River at Albany, and then a bit further on, left the interstate and headed south on Route 9 toward Kinderhook where is located the home of our 8th President, Martin Van Buren. Our tour there would include yet another unexpected connection to the life of Washington Irving.

Our docent guide was an enthusiastic college student who was very knowledgeable about President Van Buren's home, Lindenwald. She reminded us that the estate had been owned by the Van Ness family prior to President Van Buren's acquisition of the property. "And," she added as almost an afterthought, "because of the friendship of the Van Ness sons with Washington Irving, the author had been invited to reside here for an extended period of time while he was writing his *Knickerbocker's History of New York*." Once again, Washington Irving was being connected in my mind to a presidential home site.

Carol's face lit up. "You know, Clark," she said, "Irving's home is only a couple of hours south of here. Don't you think we should see it?"

"I was just thinking the same thing," I answered her quickly.

After we finished up our visit to Lindenwald and began our journey south, I tried to call to mind the next portion of Irving's biography. He had returned to the United States in 1832 to find that his books had already made him both well-known and even lionized in his own country. But his desire to visit "new scenes" and observe "strange characters and manners" had in no way been assuaged by his nearly two decades long sojourn in Europe. Now it was time to travel more widely in his own country.

The third decade of the 19th century had been a time of unparalleled western expansion in the United States. Yet there were still indigenous peoples inhabiting vast areas of the newly acquired territories, as well as physical wonders to be seen that fired the imagination.

Irving wanted to see this region before it became settled by immigrants looking for places to begin new lives in this New World, and in the very year of his return home from Europe, he set out to do so. The book that would chronicle his adventures was the next on my list, *A Tour of the Prairies*, which was published in 1835 as the largest part of a collection of travel remembrances entitled *The Crayon Miscellany*.

By the time of its publication, Washington Irving was in his early fifties. He was widely regarded as his country's most recognized literary figure, yet he had never owned a home of his own. He now decided that it was time to have a place to which he could return from his incessant wanderings, a place where he could write and happily spend the rest of his life. Traveling up the Hudson from Manhattan to the Catskill region which he had first seen as a teenager, he found a property that provided him exactly what he was looking for. It was known locally as "The Roost." Irving would rename it "Sunnyside."

His description of the property provides a perfect example of his eye for detail, his appreciation of the history of the home's setting, and the love and interest which had led him to purchase it:

About five-and-twenty miles from the ancient and renowned city of Manhattan, formerly called New Amsterdam, and vulgarly called New York, on the eastern bank of that expansion of the Hudson known among Dutch mariners of yore as the Tappan Zee, being in fact the great Mediterranean Sea of the New Netherlands, stands a little, old-fashioned stone mansion, all made up of gable ends, and as full of angles and corners as an old cocked hat...Though but of small dimensions, yet, like many small people, it is of mighty spirit, and values itself greatly on its antiquity, being one of the oldest edifices, for its size, in the whole country. (Wolfert's Roost 11)

This description, although it matches exactly the "Sunnyside" tourists visit today, did not describe the "Roost" Irving had purchased. The original dwelling was a two-room cottage which had once been part of a larger estate and dated from the mid-17th century. It was to be transformed by Washington Irving's imaginative fancies together with the technical skill of his architect, George Harvey, into the Dutch Colonial, Scottish Gothic, Tudor Revival, wisteria covered dream of architectural Romanticism that one now encounters at the end of a long and winding gravel drive.

It took more than a year for "The Roost" to be transformed into the home Irving had envisioned. As the renovation proceeded, he undertook yet another American story, one that he hoped would help defray the expenses of his building project. Its title was simply

Astoria, and it chronicled the experiences of the men hired by John Jacob Astor to establish a center for the American fur trade on the northwestern coast of the United States.

Astor had read Irving's *A Tour of the Prairies* with great interest and had offered the writer access to the entirety of the journals, diaries, letters, and papers of the men in his employ who had made the Herculean effort to attempt to settle and found Astoria at the mouth of the Columbia River in present day Oregon. The book that resulted was "a tale of hardships" (Burstein 286), but it was also a hymn of praise to America's resolve to carve out of the wilderness a new and larger world of enterprise and trade. The volume was a bestseller, became required reading in many schools, and also provided ample funds for the completion of the renovations at Sunnyside. Irving moved into this newly created haven of contemplation and beauty in the early fall of 1836. With the sole exception of one four-year period (1842-46) in which he was sent back to Spain as the United States' Foreign Minister to that country, Irving would live and work in Sunnyside for the rest of his life.

When Carol and I visited it in the summer of 2010, we purchased our tour tickets at the gift shop and then made our way down toward the house on foot. Even more spectacular than the elaborate "cottage" that finally came into view was the breathtaking vista of the Hudson River's "Tappan Zee." It was instantly apparent why Irving had chosen to settle here. The house occupied ground immediately adjacent to this beautiful expanse of water and forested hillsides on the far shore. It was a perfect and stunningly lovely setting for America's most well-known man of letters.

The house itself was swathed in foliage which made it difficult to take a picture of its entire expanse. Yet its nooks and crannies carried with them an undeniable charm as well. The home's more than half hidden exterior lent it a pervasive sense of mystery and romance that suited well the reputation of the author of "The Legend of Sleepy Hollow."

Our tour guide led us into the house through its overgrown and trellised front door. Once inside, on our immediate right was the location of Washington Irving's private study. It had been one of the two original rooms of the "Roost," but had now been thoroughly transformed into a scholar's workshop. Beautifully crafted floor to ceiling bookcases contained a plethora of volumes collected by Irving over his many years of travel and research. An elegant wooden desk and nearby extended table were obviously arranged for display, complete even with letter openers that Irving had used, but I kept imagining this space burgeoning with pages of manuscript and materials Irving would have needed to collect his notes and thoughts regarding the biographies he would produce over the next twenty years: life stories of Captain Benjamin Bonneville, Oliver Goldsmith, and Mahomet and his successors. And finally, a five-volume record of the life and times of his namesake, George Washington, the great opus to which he dedicated himself almost to the end of his days here at his beloved Sunnyside.

Of course, there was more to our tour than simply Irving's study. We also saw his bed-chamber, the parlor, the kitchen, and the dining room where, our docent reminded us, Washington loved to entertain his family and guests with the many stories he had collected over the years. We ended up on the long porch on the western side of the residence, a space that scenically overlooked the nearby Hudson River at one of its widest points.

But as I stood there with Carol and the group of the other tourists who were visiting on this day, I couldn't help noticing, right between the house and the edge of the Hudson, railroad tracks running parallel to the shore of the river. And almost on cue, a passenger train rattled past the house on its way to Albany and other points north.

"When were these railroad tracks added to the property?" I asked our docent. She smiled a very curious smile before she answered me.

"Actually, the line was added within ten years of Mr. Irving's purchase of the house," she began, "but that leads me to one of my favorite stories about him."

We all gathered around our docent, wondering just what she was going to say, and that unusual smile seemed to linger on her countenance as she spoke.

"As I'm sure you can well imagine, this addition initially made Mr. Irving quite upset. After all, the greatest glory of the home's setting is its expansive view of this section of the Hudson River. Now there would be passenger trains rushing by at all hours. Mr. Irving actually had to move his bedroom to the east side of the house just to be able to sleep without the disturbance of the passing trains. However, he decided not to let this new development spoil his love of Sunnyside. He understood the need for rapid transit between Manhattan and Albany, and he could appreciate the advance in technology the railroad represented.

"He also," she continued, "had frequent business himself in New York, and one day he left the house and walked directly down to the tracks. The station was about a ten-minute walk away, but he thought he might at least try to flag down an inbound train. Amazingly, the engineer on duty recognized him immediately and pulled the train to a stop right where Irving was standing.

"Mr. Irving explained his desire to go into town, and the engineer happily welcomed him aboard, before continuing the journey southward. And most interestingly," she added, "the engineer also stopped the train again at Sunnyside when Mr. Irving returned from town, rather than forcing him to ride all the way to the station before disembarking."

Our docent looked around again at our silent but most attentive group. "Isn't that wonderful?" she asked us. "Washington Irving was not only famous, not only literarily significant. He was loved, he was valued. Valued enough even to stop a train mid-transit, coming and going. How many authors could make a similar claim?"

As I stood on this western porch of Sunnyside, gazing out at the Hudson, I felt an odd kinship with that engineer. Like him, I had been flagged down, not by a man but by two separate presidential homes, Rutherford B. Hayes' Spiegel Grove and Martin Van Buren's Lindenwald, to interrupt my forward movement long enough to pause in order to take aboard an appreciation of the life and work of Washington Irving. What a delightful passenger he had turned out to be. And well worth stopping for.

2

Henry Wadsworth Longfellow

Our American Homer

Henry Wadsworth Longfellow's Craigie House in Cambridge, MA,

I love the United States of America. I love the persistence and resolve and determination of our people. I even love some of the faults we share as a nation, faults that on certain occasions can still manage to benefit us in the long run. The fault I'm thinking about right now is our rather myopic focus on the present moment and the immediate future. It's almost all we Americans consider with any real intensity. "Where are we now?" "What do we need to do to get us to where we want to be tomorrow?" These are the questions that transfix us and direct the vast majority of our endeavors.

The benefits of such an emphasis are obvious: much less time spent ruminating on past mistakes, much more time spent correcting and improving whatever has been unprofitable. Yet there are some downsides to this tendency as well. Our preoccupation with the present and immediate future can lead to a neglect and devaluation of some of the people and ideas that have played vital roles in our history, people and ideas instrumental in creating the nation we have become. And this leads me to the subject of this chapter: the poetry and world of Henry Wadsworth Longfellow.

By the time I was in grade school in the mid 1950's, Longfellow was no longer regarded as America's favorite poet. In fact, his verses were often the stuff of parody (Disney's *Silly Symphony* "Little Hiawatha" comes immediately to mind, and both Donald Duck and Porgy Pig had their comic versions of "The Village Blacksmith.") The fact that Longfellow had been so admired and lionized in his own day had become a matter of puzzlement to scholars of the 20th and 21st centuries. They preferred the works of Walt Whitman and Emily Dickinson as the prime examples of 19th century American verse. Longfellow's didactic sentimentality had not aged well, such scholars felt. Their final pronouncement on Longfellow's poetry was that it probably would be best enjoyed by children.

A few more forgiving literary critics still see value in his shorter poems, such as "The Tide Rises, the Tide Falls," "The Cross of Snow," and "The Day is Done," especially in their similarity to later poets' economy of language and honesty of intent in reflecting biographical truth. Several stanzas of the last poem cited above, these critics conclude, seem particularly apt expressions of Longfellow's ultimate value as a poet:

> **Come, read to me some poem,**
> **Some simple and heartfelt lay,**
> **That shall soothe this restless feeling,**
> **And banish the thoughts of day.**
>
> **Not from the grand old masters,**
> **Not from the bards sublime,**
> **Whose distant footsteps echo**
> **Through the corridors of Time...**
>
> **Read from some humbler poet,**
> **Whose songs gushed from his heart,**
> **As showers from the clouds of summer,**
> **Or tears from the eyelids start;...**

Their summaries of such poems are simple. Longfellow sees himself modestly as a "humble poet" whose verses, he hopes, may help to console the cares of any weary laborer. He makes no pretense of attaining lyric grandeur, but simply offers his readers heartfelt "songs" that can soothe the sorts of restless cares that can arise at the end of any difficult day. Such poems do have value, these critics conclude, for their gentle solace. Some may even occasionally have a line that has entered into the language as a well-known and often used expression, such as the penultimate line of his poem, "The Rainy Day": "Into each life some rain must fall..." But this, their analysis concludes, is essentially the extent of their importance as examples of early American poetry.

Yet even these somewhat positive assessments miss entirely both the nature and the importance of Longfellow's real contributions to the history of American literature. To judge more accurately his place in the pantheon of American writers, it is important to understand the moment in time in which he was to play a crucial role.

In 1807, the year of Longfellow's birth, the United States was still in its infancy as a nation. Thomas Jefferson was President. Much of Europe was still expecting the immanent collapse of this upstart, impossible experiment in republican government. Within five years the country would again be at war with Britain. And thus far, with the possible exception of the earliest satirical efforts of Washington Irving, the fledgling nation had produced no literature worthy of the attention of European readers.

Longfellow, even as a youth, seemed determined to change all that. Living with his family in a beautiful home in Portland, Maine, he early evidenced an interest in poetry and literary expression, an interest he would cultivate throughout his entire life.

Today the Wadsworth/Longfellow house still stands on its original site, but it is no longer at the edge of town and within sight of the harbor. It is now crowded by the expansion of urban buildings that dwarf the home's earlier grandeur. Built in 1785-86 by Longfellow's maternal grandfather, General Peleg Wadsworth, the home is lovingly curated by the Maine Historical Society and still bears eloquent witness to the aspirations of the boy who lived there for the first twenty-two years of his life.

When Carol and I visited in the summer of 2017, we were immediately impressed with the reverence with which the work of Longfellow was regarded by the docents. Throughout the home were original artifacts from the time of the Longfellow family's residence there, among them, rather poignantly, a modest writing desk in the Summer Dining Room at the back of the house on which Henry had written "The Rainy Day" on the occasion of his visiting the home and looking out northward from this room during inclement weather.

But to me the gem of the house lay elsewhere.

In 1814, the law office of Henry's father, Stephen, had burned to the ground. Faced with the loss of his place of business, Stephen had decided to transform a parlor in the front of the house into a temporary office where he could continue his legal practice. And to facilitate his clients' entrances and exits, he oversaw the addition of a separate entryway on the east side of the home. Directly across from this entryway, he added a small room that would be used as a waiting room for any client who could not immediately be admitted for consultation.

This room, however, was ultimately much more important to literature than it ever was to the practice of law, for it quickly became young Henry's favorite place in the house.

Young Longfellow's favorite room turned into china closet

Measuring a mere 15' by 5', this scant space could scarcely accommodate more than two or three waiting clients. But for the growing boy it provided ample room to read and write poetry without being constantly interrupted by the various activities and interests of his seven brothers and sisters. It was quiet and removed from the bustle of the house. For Henry, from the age of seven until the time of his graduation from college in 1825, it was the spot he most depended on for inspiration and contemplation. It was here that the boy had made up his mind that his destiny lay, not in the practice of law, as his father had wished for him, but in literature. It was a decision from which he never strayed.

Visitors to the house today, however, can find it difficult to decide exactly what the use of this room had been. Instead of an open space with a few chairs to accommodate waiting clients, there are shelves and cabinets installed on each of the long walls, making the room feel even more cramped and spare than it would have been otherwise.

These additions were the result of Stephen Longfellow's move back into a law office in town in 1826. The waiting room was transformed into a pantry, and the parlor law office became the family dining room.

Although Henry had spent much of the years from 1822 to 1825 in Brunswick, pursuing his undergraduate studies at Bowdoin College, upon his return to Portland, this change clearly troubled him. He commented bitterly, "My poetic career is finished...and no soft poetic ray has irradiated my heart--since the Goths and Vandals swept over the Rubicon of the 'front entry' and turned the Sanctum Sanctorum of the 'Little Room' into a China Closet."

Of course, rather than being "finished," Longfellow's "poetic career" had barely begun by 1826. While at Bowdoin, Longfellow had devoted himself to writing and the study of literature. Among his classmates was Nathaniel Hawthorne, another young man devoted to a literary life. They would become lifelong friends and admirers of each other's work. And even as the opportunities and responsibilities of his adult life led him further and further from the home of his youth, Longfellow would return often.

He never lost his love for Portland. He remembered the town vividly in his poetry as well. A few lines from "My Lost Youth" illustrate his feelings:

> **Often I think of the beautiful town**
> **That is seated by the sea;**
> **Often in thought go up and down**
> **The pleasant streets of that dear old town,**
> **And my youth comes back to me...**
>
> **I can see the breezy dome of groves,**

> The shadows of Deering's Woods;
> And the friendships old and the early loves
> Come back with a Sabbath sound, as of doves
> In quiet neighborhoods.

But, however clearly etched in his memory, Portland represented the past for Longfellow. His future—and his literary destiny—lay elsewhere. He was determined to become much more than the "humble poet" of "The Day is Done." He felt somewhere within himself stirrings that would transform him into the model of a new type of "grand old master," perhaps even of a "bard sublime." And to that end, his stars were about to align themselves.

Just a year after his graduation from Bowdoin College, Longfellow was invited to join its faculty as a professor of Modern Languages. To be prepared for his work, however, he would need to travel to Europe to hone his linguistic skills. He did so with gusto, traveling extensively across the continent and gaining a working knowledge of seven languages during this period. By the time he returned to Maine to begin his professorial duties in 1829, he had immersed himself in the beauty and classic literature of Europe. He had also readied himself to write the poetry for which he would ultimately be awarded the acclaim of the world.

But not before facing some significant trials in his life. Initially all seemed to be going well. Two years after he had assumed his duties at Bowdoin, he married a childhood friend, Mary Storer Potter. The couple lived in Brunswick until 1834 when an offer came to Henry from Harvard University near Boston to oversee the Modern Languages program there. He readily accepted the offer, and he also agreed to Harvard's stipulation that, before commencing his new position, he would return to Europe to further his linguistic studies. In 1835 he and Mary departed Brunswick for this new adventure.

And now for the first time in his life Henry experienced a deep personal tragedy. Within months of the Longfellows' arrival in Europe, Mary became seriously ill. She died before the year was out, leaving her young husband alone and devastated. Henry quickly slipped into a dark melancholy. Only his work kept him from total despair. He plunged into his studies with an ardent fervor and labored tirelessly to become more knowledgeable and, most particularly, to master German.

It was eight months before his aspect brightened a bit. He was traveling in Switzerland at the time when he introduced himself to the family of Nathan Appleton, a wealthy industrialist and member of the most prestigious circles of Boston society. Mr. Appleton was traveling with his two daughters, Mary and 19-year-old Frances ("Fanny"). Longfellow was almost immediately attracted to Fanny, but she, eleven years his junior, felt no real interest in becoming attached to a minor poet and Harvard academic. His romantic interest in her was unreturned. Nevertheless, despite this initial failure, Henry had once again felt the warmth and joy of love, however unrequited. He returned home to New England in December of 1836 ready to assume his new duties at Harvard.

To do so, however, he had to find a place to live. His first rented room became unacceptable to him by the end of the academic year. The location he chose next would forever alter his life and his literary fortunes.

He found himself applying to rent a room in the so-called "Craigie House" on Brattle Street, quite near the University. In fact, Mrs. Craigie, a financially strapped widow, had often rented rooms in her spacious home to gentlemen employed at Harvard. Initially she balked at Longfellow's application because she supposed him to be an undergraduate, but he soon convinced her that, despite his youth, he was both a widower and the new director of the Modern Languages department. He moved in by the summer of 1837.

For a talented young poet desirous of making a name both for himself and for his country's literature, this was a most fortunate address. "Craigie House" had also been the residence of George Washington for almost a year during the siege of Boston in 1775. Washington, along with numerous luminaries of the Revolutionary War, had worked out military strategies in the very rooms where Longfellow was beginning to write poetry which featured pictures of American life and glimpses of heretofore unsung heroes and heroines of the New World.

He published his first book of poetry in 1839. In 1841 his second volume of poems *Ballads and Other Poems* enjoyed an immediate popular success and included such memorable works as "The Wreck of the Hesperus" and "The Village Blacksmith."

By 1843 even Longfellow's fortunes in love had taken a turn for the better. Perhaps because of his growing reputation and success as a writer, and perhaps because the perspective of a twenty-six-year-old unmarried woman differed markedly from that of a girl of nineteen, Fanny Appleton wrote Henry an encouraging note urging him to come visit her. The couple were married in August of the same year.

As a wedding gift for his daughter and new son-in-law, Nathan Appleton purchased Craigie House where Henry had been living as a boarder for six years. Henry and Fanny Longfellow now owned the entire property. Within the next four years, Fanny would give birth to three children, the first of six, and Henry would produce a work that would make him the most revered poet in the United States: "Evangeline."

When I first encountered this remarkable poem in 2017, it was a revelation to me. To start with, it treated a chapter of American history of which I had been completely unaware, the "Great Upheaval" of 1755 when Britain had forcibly removed thousands of French colonists from their Acadian homes during the French and Indian war. But more than being an interesting history lesson, it was also a moving and poignant account of separated lovers, each faithfully searching to reunite with the other. It was much longer than most poems, well over a thousand lines, and lastly, it was written in a meter totally unfamiliar to me, at least so I thought upon my first reading.

> **This is the forest primeval; but where are the hearts that beneath it**
> **Leaped like the roe, when he hears in the woodland the voice of the huntsman?**
> **...Naught but tradition remains of the beautiful village of Grand-Pre.**

This was certainly unlike any Longfellow I had read before, but as image led on to image and episode to episode, I found myself both following and envisioning the story being told. I also began scanning the lines metrically and discovered a pattern of rough dactylic hexameter: /uu/uu/uu/uu/uu/u. This was odd. Poets writing in English almost always choose iambic rising metric feet (u/) rather than trochaic and dactylic falling metric feet (/u or /uu). The rising rhythm fits the English language much better. So why was Longfellow choosing to write in this much more difficult meter—and at such length?

And then it hit me. Dactylic hexameter is a rare rhythm in English poetry, but it was precisely the meter of both *The Iliad* and *The Odyssey*. The Greek language lends itself perfectly to the metrics of a falling rhythm, but it also stands for the timeless standard of classic literature. Longfellow was announcing to the world that an American literature was being born, classical in form but completely indigenous in subject matter. He had assumed the poetic mantle of an American Homer.

He had done so in the most auspicious of locales. Since his and Fanny's acquisition of Craigie House, Henry had claimed as his study the large downstairs parlor to the immediate right of the front door.

Longfellow's Study in Craigie House

Aside from the appeal of its open interior with floor to ceiling bookcases and ample space for an expansive writing table, this was also the very room which George Washington had chosen as his headquarters during the early days of the American Revolution. In this room Washington had made decisions that ultimately would earn for him the title of "Father of His Country." In this room Longfellow would produce over the course of the next ten years works that would identify him as America's most widely read and revered poet.

His next poetic narrative would expand and build upon the foundation established by "Evangeline." It would be over five times as long, a work of epic length and scope. Yet it too would come to be misinterpreted, even misunderstood, by readers of the 20th century. Longfellow spent nearly seven years researching, writing, rewriting, and testing it out on friends and relations. Written in the falling rhythmic meter of an Indian drumbeat (trochaic tetrameter), *The Song of Hiawatha* would be his masterpiece. From its very opening lines, the poet establishes the almost limitless canvas of the uniquely American backdrop of the work to come:

> Should you ask me, whence these stories?
> Whence these legends and traditions,
> With the odors of the forest,
> With the dew and damp of meadows,
> With the curling smoke of wigwams,
> With the rushing of great rivers,
> With their frequent repetitions,
> And their wild reverberations,
> As of thunder in the mountains?
>
> I should answer, I should tell you,
> "From the forests and the prairies,
> From the great lakes of the North-land,
> From the land of the Ojibways,
> From the land of the Dacotahs,
> From the mountains, moors, and fen-lands,
> Where the heron, the Shuh-shuh-gah,
> Feeds among the reeds and rushes.
> I repeat them as I heard them
> From the lips of Nawadaha,
> The musician, the sweet singer."

The tale, which is then told over the course of more than a hundred pages, recounts the birth, childhood, marriage, tragedies, and epic conquests of Hiawatha, a half-god, half-man, Indian. He is, of course, no more historically real than Odysseus or Achilles of the Greek epics, yet he, like those earlier figures, comes to personify and illustrate the values and beauty of the people he has been created to represent. And, certainly a rarity in the American literature of its day, an Indian figure was being presented not as a cunning and dangerous adversary, but rather as an ideal hero, worthy both of respect and emulation.

The poem was a huge success, selling, by Longfellow's best estimates, over 50,000 copies in the first two years of its publication.

The little boy from Portland had become America's most well-known and beloved poet. He had done so through a synthesis of Old-World literary techniques and New World characters and content. An American author, his work demonstrated, should be taken seriously. And, as if in confirmation of that fact, in 1884, two years after his death, Longfellow would be the first American writer to be honored with a memorial bust in the famed Poets' Corner of Westminster Abbey.

After the success of *The Song of Hiawatha*, Longfellow continued his exploration of American history by returning to the heroic meter of *Evangeline* in a new epic work, *The Courtship of Miles Standish*. Here, however, his research took on a more personal tone as the mother's side of his family traced its lineage back to Priscilla and John Alden. The poem told the story of a Cyrano de Bergerac type love triangle (though written fifty years *before* the famous play by Rostand), and was another marked success for Longfellow, selling more than 25,000 copies in the United States (and 10,000 copies in a single day in London). It would be his final extended poetic narrative.

In 1861, Longfellow's life once again turned tragic. Fanny's dress caught fire while she was playing with two of their children. Henry, who was in the next room, rushed to his wife's aid and finally managed to put out the flames that had engulfed her. It was too late for Fanny, however. She died the next morning from the injuries she had sustained. Henry, too, had been severely burned during his efforts to save his wife. His face was so badly scarred that, even after his wounds had healed, he decided never to shave again. The resultant beard became the trademark feature of his later years.

He was, for the second time in his life, disconsolate, and he now needed to concentrate on raising his children as a single parent. Creative work seemed no longer a possibility.

Nevertheless, with one last gargantuan effort, he managed to cobble together a number of poetic narratives he had been working on for several years into a final lengthy work that he originally titled *The Sudbury Tales*, a clear reference to the famous *Canterbury Tales* of Geoffrey Chaucer. Like that earlier work, the premise of Longfellow's collection of poetic stories is that a group of travelers find themselves all spending the night at an old country inn. (The inn that served as the work's setting still stands and features a front parlor room decorated just as it is described in Longfellow's text.) The members of this gathering of diverse American types decide to spend the evening entertaining each other by telling stories. The Landlord's Tale, the first tale told, is the famous "Paul Revere's Ride." Released finally as *Tales of a Wayside Inn* in 1863, the book sold well, but was Longfellow's last attempt to produce an original American narrative.

The Wayside Inn in Sudbury, MA

Yet what a success Longfellow's literary efforts had been. He had achieved both the prominence he had desired since boyhood and had managed to convince a worldwide reading audience of the worth, even the excellence, of literature produced in the New World. So why has his poetry become so lowered in the esteem of modern scholars? This was the question for which I had failed to find a satisfactory answer prior to visiting his Cambridge home with Carol in the summer of 2017.

We had arrived by train from Concord and had walked the several blocks from Harvard Square down Brattle Street to the location of Craigie House. It sits well back from the road, and we were immediately impressed with the obvious care taken to preserve and maintain the home in its original condition. Now identified as the Longfellow House Washington's Headquarters National Park Site, visitors enter the property from Brattle Street and walk to the left around the home to the official park entrance. Once inside the small shop and waiting area, we paid our admission and met others in our tour group when a Park Ranger joined us. She had us stow our belongings in a nearby closet and then asked us, "Are you more interested in Washington or in Longfellow today?"

Clearly the majority of our group's answer would affect the content of her presentation. Happily, we all agreed that we were equally interested in both men.

Our guide, a young woman I will call Susan, was both knowledgeable and appreciative of the significance of this site. Her chief interest lay in history, however, more than in literature, and many of her observations about Longfellow during the tour concentrated more on his early support of the abolitionist movement and his close friendship with the firebrand senator from Massachusetts, Charles Sumner, than on any of the poetry he had written here.

One notable exception to this emphasis occurred in Longfellow's bedroom. Susan quite pointedly called the group's attention to the delicately drawn portrait of Fanny Appleton Longfellow hanging opposite the bed, and she referred to his poignant poem written twenty years after her tragic and premature death, "The Cross of Snow."

Overall, both Carol and I were very glad that we had come to see the home, but I wanted to ask Susan an additional question. The group dispersed, and Susan came up to me and asked if I needed any more information about the house.

"No," I answered her, "not about the house. But I do have one more question. How do you feel about Longfellow's poetry?"

She looked at me, pausing a moment before she spoke. But then quite forcibly answered, "Frankly, my only wish is that no one would read *The Song of Hiawatha* anymore." I was surprised and quickly asked her why she felt as she did.

"Because I have friends with Native American backgrounds, and they have assured me that the poem is not based on reality. It mixes up traditions of various tribes, and it's a myth that doesn't tell the truth about Indian life and values. I really wish people wouldn't read it."

I could tell that this was a sensitive matter to her, so I thanked Susan for her tour of the home and exited out onto the lawn again to find Carol.

It took me quite a while to process this brief interchange. Initially I felt a little disheartened by her response, yet I was also impressed with the clarity and courage of her answer. And then I suddenly realized that I was seeing the matter only from my own perspective, the point of view of an English teacher who had recently discovered the enormous worth of a writer he had previously neglected. What could Susan's perspective teach me? And what could it tell me about the larger problem of Longfellow's current position in the pantheon of American writers?

An answer that presented itself to me was the insight with which I began this chapter. Americans tend to focus on the present moment and the needs of the immediate future. Susan had personal friends with legitimate concerns about today's Native Americans. As a result, she wanted people to have a clear and honest picture of the complex realities of Indian life, including the injustices Native Americans had suffered over the years. Only then could social progress be made. In that context, for Susan at least, Longfellow's poetry was no help at all and perhaps was an actual hindrance to bringing about necessary change.

But Longfellow's goal had been to legitimize American literature, to prove to the world that both our writers and our people were worthy of any reader's attention. And to that end he had been extraordinarily successful. Yet for Susan, and perhaps for a great number of today's Americans, such a goal no longer seemed relevant to the present moment. We do not question ourselves as to our worth in the world. We speak of The American Century and American Exceptionalism, and we often pride ourselves on the character and resilience of our people.

Has Longfellow's poetry, then, simply outlived its relevance to a nation so consistently focused on current needs and the immediate future?

It may be worthy of noting that, to some degree, the works of Homer have suffered a similar fate. When he was composing his epics, he, like Longfellow, was writing during what later scholars would identify as a "Dark Age" in Greek history, the 7th or 8th century BCE. Both Homer and Longfellow were looking into the past to create enduring monuments to the qualities and character they saw latent in their own people, qualities which if appreciated and cultivated, could lead them into the greatness of which they were capable. But it took Homer's descendants two or three centuries for that greatness to flower into Greece's Golden Age of the 5th century BCE.

What if America's greatest moments in history, similarly, are yet to be achieved? If so, perhaps it is worth our while to pay closer attention to some of Longfellow's observations and insights into the strengths of the American people. It could be that his words, like Homer's to the Greeks of his day, could play a key role in encouraging and inspiring us to achieve the sort of success that modern Americans most desire.

There is an oft-repeated story that, late in his life, Longfellow answered a knock on the door of Craigie house to find a young admirer of his poetry standing before him. The woman, not recognizing him and assuming he was a servant, asked, "Is this the house where Mr. Longfellow was born?" When he told her that it was not, she asked, "Then is this the house where he died?"

"Not yet," was his simple reply.

My hope is that his answer can continue to remain true. Henry Wadsworth Longfellow deserves both an active readership and a living place in the history of our nation's literature. He was, and is, our American Homer.

3

Ralph Waldo Emerson

"The Sun Shines To-day Also"

The Old Manse in Concord, MA

It had happened here. Well, it had started here at least. And, as a result, the philosophical and intellectual landscape of the United States would be forever altered. In October of 1834, just up these stairs in a small room on the second floor that once had been a study for a family line of ministers, Ralph Waldo Emerson placed a writing desk near one of the room's three windows. It afforded the young man a view of a storied location: the ground where the Old North Bridge once stood and where, in April 1775, a colonial militia first repulsed British soldiers marching toward Concord, Massachusetts, and its store of munitions.

Emerson's minister grandfather, William, and his family had watched the battle unfold from these very windows, and soon thereafter William would volunteer to act as a chaplain in Washington's Continental Army.

But Ralph Waldo was not looking longingly back to the glorious era of the American Revolution as he gazed out across the now quiet fields bordering the gently flowing waters of the Concord River nearby. Despite whatever hallowed historical memories may have lingered in this place, Emerson had come to understand that there was yet another, even greater, revolution to be fought and won. Historical events, he now believed, were merely precursors of this greater revolutionary cause toward which he was now beginning to apply his talents and determination: a revolution of thought and vision, a revolution that would free American thinkers and writers from the philosophical, literary, and religious strictures imposed upon them by the examples and assumptions of European models. For Emerson, rejecting the political colonialism of the Old World was only the beginning. The real challenge before this new nation was the rejection of intellectual colonialism, replacing it with spiritual, literary, and philosophical ideas that had never yet been thought or spoken.

And here in the second floor study of the Old Manse, Emerson devoted his energies to providing for this great new cause the same sort of explanatory and provocative document that a young Thomas Jefferson had labored to write in the second story room he had occupied in Philadelphia in 1776. Jefferson had struggled to create a document which would stir the hearts and minds of those who read or heard it to rise up in active support of its ideals. The results of his efforts he named The Declaration of Independence.

Emerson's declaration bore a simpler title, though its effects were arguably every bit as far reaching as had been Jefferson's. Here in his second floor study, Emerson announced the birth of a new form of thinking, a transcendental philosophy based on the principles of self-reliance and the inherent worthiness of all men. What he began to write here was a direct challenge to almost all the European models that had preceded it. The extended essay that resulted carried only one word as its title: *Nature*.

Right from its opening page Emerson sounded a call for a profound change in the way citizens of the New World should be thinking and expressing themselves. It was a theme he would restate and pursue over the entire course of his intellectual life. One can imagine him, poised, pen in hand, sitting at his modest desk and gazing out on the landscape just outside his window. Remembering the Revolutionary history enacted here fifty-nine years earlier, he began to speak both forcefully and compellingly:

> *Our age is retrospective. It builds the sepulchers of the fathers. It writes biographies, histories, and criticism. The foregoing generations beheld God and nature face to face, we, through their eyes. Why should not we also enjoy an original relation to the universe? Why should not we have a poetry and philosophy of insight and not of tradition, and religion by revelation to us, and not the history of theirs?...The sun shines to-day also...There are new lands, new men, new thoughts. Let us demand our own works and laws and worship. (3)*

The tendency of the current age, he began, is to look back at whatever has already been accomplished. We attempt to understand only the lives and stories of those who have previously distinguished themselves. We examine the relative worth or fallacies of their discoveries. Any spiritual insights they may have gleaned we can comprehend only by trying to see the truth through the lens of their perspective.

Then suddenly, Emerson turns toward his readers with a penetrating question. Is it not possible for modern men to achieve for themselves the heights reached by earlier poets, philosophers, and prophets? In answering his own question, he then sounds the theme of his entire work. Yes, he assures us. There is as much light, as much truth, as many revelations still available to contemporary searchers for inspiration as there ever were in human history. It remains up to his readers, to those of his own generation, to demand the right to find them.

This was a startling pronouncement on the part of this young man, still relatively unknown in the world. He had attended Harvard but had graduated with only middling success. On occasion he had taught school, but had never made any serious attempt to become a career educator. Emerson had returned to Harvard, this time entering the Divinity School to prepare himself for a ministerial position. However, he was sickly and afraid his life might be cut short before he accomplished anything of note. What, then, could explain the force and certainty that underlay both the questions and the affirmations of these introductory words of his tract?

The events of 1826-1834, the nine years immediately preceding his move to Concord and his residence in the Old Manse, cast a telling light onto the assertions of Emerson's powerful opening paragraph.

By the summer of 1826, he had completed his formal education, both at Harvard and at its Divinity School. Regarding his Harvard years, he remarked that "I was the true philosopher in college and they [his professors] the false." After his training in the Divinity School, he noted in his journal that "The profession [the ministry] is antiquated. In an altered age, we worship in the dead forms of our forefathers....I have sometimes thought that, in order to be a good minister, it was necessary to leave the ministry." Such braggadocio and such musings are not uncommon among scholars who have not yet managed to distinguish themselves. Thus, it is important to regard these early journal entries with a certain amount of skepticism. Nevertheless, it is clear the young Emerson was thinking deeply about himself and about the path in life he desired to pursue.

He was also deeply concerned about his own ill health. Fearing the onset of consumption, a disease that ultimately would claim the lives of several members of his family, Emerson heeded his doctor's advice to seek a warmer climate during the winter months. In late November of 1826, he boarded a ship bound for Charleston, South Carolina.

Charleston, however, would turn out to be a disappointment. South Carolina was experiencing an unusually bitter winter that year, and because of this it failed to provide the respite his frail health required. But Emerson had heard that St. Augustine, a town in the northern section of the recently acquired state of Florida, had much more temperate weather and particularly healthful air. He decided to proceed further south and hope for the best. This decision would play a significant role not only in bettering his health, but, even more importantly, in encouraging his progress as a thinker, writer, and philosopher.

Before any such developments could occur, however, Emerson would need to face his most immediate problem: the fact that for the first time in his life he was completely alone. This trip south had been a decision made in desperation. Forced to borrow money for his passage, he had no additional means with which to pay the fare for a companion. With neither family nor friends to comfort him, and possessed of (or burdened by) a naturally reticent temperament, Emerson realized that whatever healing there was to be had in St. Augustine, it would have to depend upon his own determination, his own self-reliance.

St. Augustine in 1826 was unlike any town Emerson had ever known. In fact, it was unlike any other town in the United States. It had been founded in the 16th century by the Spanish to help protect their gold fleet sailing from South and Central America up the Gulf Stream along the coast of Florida before crossing the Atlantic en route to Spain. In the 18th century, the town had been ceded to Great Britain at the close of the Seven Years' war. Twenty years later it had been returned to Spain as part of the Treaty of Paris that concluded the American Revolution. Most recently the United States had acquired it from Spain, along with the rest of the Florida peninsula, in 1821.

St. Augustine's population was comprised of a disparate group of peoples, reflecting the ever-changing status of its over 250-year-old history. Minorcans constituted the largest segment of its citizens, but there were also Indians, both freed and enslaved blacks, and others who, for a variety of reasons, had simply drifted into the area and taken root there. Catholicism was the dominant religion, but there was also a small Protestant presence, though quite unlike the Unitarian church with which Emerson was familiar.

The buildings throughout St. Augustine, many of them in various states of ruin, were older than any structures Emerson had ever seen, and the lifestyle of the people there seemed unconscionably lazy. He remarked in a letter sent to his brother William in late January, "What is done here? Nothing" (Griffin 120). Yet witnessing the listlessness of the local population seemed to strengthen Emerson's own resolve to make something of himself. He visited both the town's Catholic and Protestant churches, but found each spiritually wanting. Ever mindful of his physical condition, he began to pace himself, leaving no time either for inaction nor for overaction. He began writing poetry and taking long walks around the town. And with each passing week he felt himself becoming stronger and more resolute.

Then, toward the end of his stay in St. Augustine, Emerson made the acquaintance of Prince Napoleon Achille Marat, a nephew of Napoleon Bonaparte. This encounter, would turn out to be a most consequential event. Exactly how the two men met is still a matter of debate. Tradition suggests that Marat and his wife of nine months may have rented a room in the same house in which Emerson had set up residence. That house still stands in a corner lot of a quiet street in the old town, though it is not currently open to visitors. But neither Marat nor Emerson were planning to stay very long in St. Augustine. As winter was over and his health had significantly improved, Emerson was scheduled first to return to Charleston and then back north to New England. The Marats were also traveling to Charleston, after which they had booked passage on a south bound ship headed to their home in Western Florida. They all boarded the same boat bound for

Charleston for what was supposed to be a three-day cruise. However, tempestuous weather, while not seriously endangering their vessel, considerably delayed its progress. The voyage took nine days before they finally arrived in South Carolina and were able to disembark. But by that time, Emerson and Marat had cemented what each man regarded as a lifelong friendship.

Emerson wrote in his journal:

> *I have connected myself by friendship to a man who with as ardent a love of truth as that which animates me, with a mind surpassing mine in the variety of its research, and sharpened and strengthened to an energy for action to which I have no pretense…is, yet,…a consistent atheist—and a disbeliever in the existence, and, of course, the immortality of the soul. (Griffin 126)*

Achilles Marat, two years older and considerably more traveled than Emerson, was unlike anyone he had encountered in St. Augustine. He was well-read, a scholar with an active mind, and an "ardent [lover] of truth." One can only imagine how welcome Emerson must have found such a man with such a spirit in this town. What a contrast he must have made to the lackadaisical tendencies of the majority of the population here. Emerson had always admired Napoleon Bonaparte for his tireless energy. In years to come, he would write that Napoleon was "…never weak and literary, but [he] acts with the solidity and the precision of natural agents" (*Representative Men* 218). He recognized and admired this same quality, this "energy for action" in Achilles Marat.

According to the notes each made after their nine-day cruise to Charleston, both men agreed that they had spent most of their time in an almost ceaseless series of conversations. They debated political ideas, disagreed on key social issues of the day (most notably those regarding slavery), and discussed their opposing views of religion, Marat being an insistent and unrepentant atheist.

Yet through all the sturm und drang of both the weather and their contrasting opinions, the two men thoroughly enjoyed the other's company and ended up appreciating the other's point of view. For perhaps the first time in his life, Emerson had found an intellect with whom he could engage in vigorous debate and still manage to hold his own. Though he had earlier doubted his ability to demonstrate the "energy for action" that he so admired in both Napoleon and Marat, this voyage attested to the fact that his earlier timidity was being replaced with a strengthened conviction in the validity and defensibility of his own set of ideals. The two men would never meet again, but Emerson recorded in a journal entry the spirit of his newfound enthusiasm:

> *I lead a new life. I occupy new ground in the world of the spirits, untenanted before. I commence a career of thought and action which is expanding before me into a distant and dazzling infinity. (Griffin 128)*

Of course, such youthful exuberance would have to undergo severe tests in the years to come. Still, there are many reasons to agree with historian Patricia C. Griffin who concluded that "He left New England a youth and came back from St. Augustine a man." (128)

In 1827, the year he returned from St. Augustine, Emerson's personal life also seemed to take a marked turn for the better. On Christmas Day of that year he met Ellen Louisa Tucker, a wealthy and attractive girl about eight years his junior. He fell instantly in love with her. Before the following Christmas, the couple was officially engaged, and they celebrated their wedding in September of 1829.

By this time Emerson's professional life had also improved. Inspired by both his healthier constitution and by his strengthened self-confidence, Emerson applied for and was offered a position in the prestigious Second Unitarian Church in Boston. By July of 1829, he had been named its pastor, a post which came with a salary of $1,800 a year, a considerable sum in those days.

But his happiness was short-lived. After only a few months of married life, Ellen fell seriously ill. Emerson's mother moved in with the young couple to help care for her daughter-in-law, but after a very difficult year, Ellen died in early February of 1831. They had not yet celebrated their second anniversary.

Emerson was devastated. He had lost the love of his life. At the age of 29, he was once again alone.

And equally crushing to him was the fact that his religion seemed not to hold the solace for which he desperately yearned. For the next year, concerns from his earlier Harvard days flooded back into his mind: Where was Truth to be found? Why was he overseeing religious rituals "in the dead forms" of previous ages, rituals in which he no longer believed and which, furthermore, he felt Jesus himself had never intended to be made permanent elements of Christian worship?

Emerson wrote and delivered a sermon on this controversial topic, and soon thereafter, on December 22, 1832, tendered his resignation.

Three days later, on Christmas Day, he boarded a ship bound for Europe. Perhaps there he would find answers to the doubts and uncertainties that haunted him. And he knew precisely the people he wanted to question. He recorded in his journal that "my narrow and desultory reading had inspired the wish to see the faces of three or four writers,--Coleridge, Wordsworth, [Walter Savage]

Landor,...and the latest and strongest contributor to the critical journals, Carlyle."

He spent ten months of the year 1833 in Europe doing precisely that. Starting in Italy and ending his travels in England, he met all of these men and thoroughly enjoyed his conversations with them. Yet his journal entries after these travels revealed a surprising conclusion: "...after allowing myself freely to be dazzled by the various brilliancy of men of talent--in calm hours I found myself no way helped..." "I thank the great God who has led me through this European scene, this last schoolroom in which he has pleased to instruct me...He has shown me the men I wished to see...[All four—Landor, Coleridge, Wordsworth, and Carlyle—were deficient] in insight into religious truth. They have no idea of that species of moral truth which I call the first philosophy. [God] has thereby comforted and confirmed me in my convictions."

Emerson found himself to be the intellectual equal of the greatest minds in contemporary Europe. Though temporarily "dazzled" by the intelligence and articulateness of their conversations, he came away from the time he spent with these men feeling spiritually empty. Clearly there was a place for him in the world. He felt himself being led to a philosophical and spiritual calling to which not one of these great writers and thinkers had yet laid claim.

This, then, was the Ralph Waldo Emerson who returned to America in 1834. The man who would sit in the second floor study of the Old Manse in Concord and confidently and forcefully begin the essay that would forever change the intellectual landscape of his nation. He had been educated. He had mastered his own physical weakness. He had found himself able to debate and defend his ideas. He had weathered deep personal loss. He had met the great minds of Europe and had found his own insights spiritually superior to theirs. Now it was time for him to teach.

Emerson's "Bush" in Concord, MA

In May of 1834 he received a sizable settlement from the estate of his deceased wife and, by June of the following year, he was able to buy a house nearer to the center of town. It sat on two acres of land and included a separate barn. Emerson would come to call it "Bush," and it would serve him well as a center of his life and thought. On September 15, 1835, he welcomed his new wife, Lydian Jackson, here, along with his mother. He enlarged the home, creating a workroom and study on the first floor, with an entire wall crowded "with many books and papers." And in this newly created haven of thought and enterprise, he revised and completed *Nature* which would appear in print for the first time in 1836. This would be his home for the rest of his life. He and Lydian would have four children born here, and the front room workroom and study would become the center of intellectual life in Concord.

The home still stands and is run by the Ralph Waldo Emerson Memorial Association. When Carol and I last visited in the summer of 2016, our guide met us at the front door of the home and immediately indicated that we should turn to the right and be seated in the first floor study.

What an experience it was to realize that we had joined a very prestigious group of people who had come here over the years to listen to and speak with "the sage of Concord." His personal friends, of course, included Bronson and Louisa May Alcott, Nathaniel and Sophia Hawthorne, and Henry David Thoreau. All these people were his neighbors. But many visitors from further afield had also come to be a part of the revolution of thought and expression for which Emerson had called in the opening paragraph of *Nature*.

Fellow poets James Russell Lowell and Walt Whitman had discussed poetry with Emerson in this room. Activists John Brown and Horace Mann had each debated here the causes they championed. David Chester French, the famous sculptor of the Minute Man statue erected close to the Old North Bridge, had come to work on a sculpture of Emerson himself, and the naturalist John Muir who had met Emerson in California and described him as "...the most...sequoia-like soul I ever met" had come here eleven years after Emerson's death simply to have the honor of placing flowers on his grave.

Perhaps no one expressed more perfectly the feeling of being in this place than one of Emerson's most frequent visitors: Margaret Fuller. This firebrand of feminist causes, who had spent more than forty days in residence here in the room across the hall from the study, declared that walking into Emerson's "Bush" was like "entering a paradise of thought."

And here we were, listening to our guide, gazing up at the imposing wall of books on the room's inner wall, and looking at the circular writing table in the middle of the room where Emerson used to sit in a rocking chair. Here he would welcome visitors and, when left to himself, would write his "Self-Reliance," "The American Scholar," and "The Over-Soul," together with books, including *Essays: First Series*, *Essays: Second Series*, *Representative Men*, and *Conduct of Life*. One feels a distinct sense of honor in being invited to sit here and remember the extraordinary intellectual events that transpired in this very room.

(Author's Note: The actual study that had occupied this space in the home is no longer located here. What visitors encounter is an admirable replica of that original room which was given to the nearby Concord Museum for safe-keeping and has been reassembled there as an important exhibit.)

In a journal entry he made following his 1833 grand tour of Europe, Emerson had written, "I am very glad my traveling is done." One wonders if he ever came to see just how ironic this sentiment would prove to be. Though Emerson would always return to his beloved "Bush," he would spend the rest of his life traveling the country and lecturing, encouraging and energizing his listeners to appreciate the worthiness of their own unique discoveries. He would give over a thousand lectures and would write hundreds of letters of encouragement and counsel to those who sought his aid and advice. He was a generous man and a faithful friend. When Bronson Alcott needed money with which to purchase a home for his family, Emerson advanced it to him. When Bronson's daughter, Louisa May, showed her aptitude as a young writer, Emerson opened his library of books to her. When Henry David Thoreau, in his pursuit of Truth, wished to live a life of simplicity by the shores of Walden Pond, Emerson gladly allowed him to build his cabin on land he owned there.

Ralph Waldo Emerson was more than "the sage of Concord," more even than "the Passive Master" referred to on his tombstone. He was also the great lender of "his hand to the Vast Soul" which he saw at work in the genius of the men and women he knew and loved. His appreciation and encouragement of this new generation of writers, artists, and thinkers may be his greatest and most ongoing legacy.

4

Henry David Thoreau

The Dipper, The Rosetta Stone, and Birdsong

Walden Pond in Concord, MA

Walden Pond in Concord, MA

"Carol," I began, "do we have a list of the names of my students from the last several years?"

This was an unusual question, and Carol, always wary of such inquiries, had a quick answer.

"What are you thinking about, sweetheart?" she asked. "I'm sure we could come up with one if we needed to have it."

"Well, I believe I owe those kids a partial refund—at least a gesture of some kind."

"Why?" was her next obvious question.

"Because," I began, " after my most recent reading of *Walden*, I realize that although I've taught that amazing book to my American Lit students for a couple of years now, I had never fully understood it. I hadn't grasped the scope of its genius. And I was wondering if a small rebate would ease the guilt I'm feeling now."

Carol, our intrepid budget maker, gave me a hug and smiled.

"Do you understand the book now?" she asked gently.

"Not entirely. Thoreau's allusions run a huge gamut of knowledge. But I do finally appreciate its essential points, its poetry, and its profound wisdom."

"Well, as your wife and as our money manager, I can say that rebates aren't possible right now. But if you take this new knowledge and enthusiasm into the next class you're assigning *Walden*, I believe you'll be doing everything you need to do."

As always, Carol was right. So let me now be as clear as I can possibly be. I believe that *Walden* is the most important book ever written by an American particularly for Americans. This is **not** to say that it the most important book ever written. Nor is it a book written **exclusively** for Americans. However, within its pages, Henry David Thoreau, the Massachusetts born author of *Walden*, wrestled with a host of fundamental questions that had a special importance for his immediate audience: the 19th century literate population of his country, a nation that had existed for less than a century at the time he was writing. The fact that his questions continue to challenge and relate to his country's 21st century readers only confirms the power of his insight into the American character.

And just what **are** these fundamental questions? Let me list a few of them. What is essential to my existence, and what is inessential? How do I discover a meaningful purpose to my life? Does Truth exist? If so, where can I find it? What role does the natural world play in my efforts to find answers to these questions?

I call these questions essentially "American" not out of any jingoistic pride in my country, but because, in the New World, such questions were already in the hearts and minds of many of the people who had come to live here. Not necessarily in the conscious thoughts of the first wave of immigrants. Their concerns were mostly centered on simple survival. But once these pioneers had established a foothold in this new and, to them at least, virtually endless continent, they, and more certainly their descendants, faced the host of questions mentioned above. Why? Because these people had chosen to start life over again—from its very beginning. They had no thousand-year-old heritage around them, filled with agreed upon answers to the basic questions of life. They had no predetermined social classes, no assumed political order. And they were surrounded by nature, a nature not the product of carefully groomed gardens and laid-out plots of land, but an overwhelming, encroaching nature that both provided them with vital materials for living and at the same time threatened to annihilate them with cataclysms of unimaginably powerful elemental forces.

In such a context, the issue of what was and was not essential for life became vitally important. And then arose the question of one's individual purpose. Why am I here? Is there a Truth to be found in this wilderness? Is Nature an ally or an adversary or both? No book written by an American had ever addressed such questions with the thoroughness and courage that Thoreau brought to the pages of *Walden*. And yet the man himself was one of the most unassuming visionaries imaginable.

"I have travelled a good deal in Concord..."

Scholars tend to see these words from the opening chapter of *Walden* as being indicative of the expansive range of Thoreau's thought as he lived and worked within the physical confines of the area surrounding his home town. However, this statement was also literally true. The Thoreau family resided in no fewer than eight separate homes in Concord during Henry's lifetime, not including the years when Henry would choose to live alone by the shore of Walden pond.

The Thoreau birthplace still stands, though not in its original location. John Thoreau, Henry's father, married the daughter of Mary Minot, a widow who had inherited a farm near the town of Concord. Minot had no interest in occupying this property herself, however, and so she asked her daughter and new son-in-law to work the farm in exchange for providing them with a place in which to live. John and Cynthia attempted to make the farm turn a profit, but they were unable to do so. The one bright spot in the time of their residence here was the birth of their son Henry in July of 1817. However, by the end of the following spring, the family moved out, and after a brief stay with Mrs. Minot, left Concord for a space of five years.

Thoreau's Birthplace, Concord, MA

Upon their return in 1823, John began his pencil-making business, and the Thoreau family resided in several rental houses in town between 1823 and 1834.

Concord's Colonial Inn

By the time Henry was attending Harvard, the family had moved again, this time to a location that had been passed down by Henry's paternal grandfather. This structure still stands and now constitutes the eastern most wing of the Concord Colonial Inn on Monument Street and is located at the north end of the square in the center of town. The family shared this residence with two aunts, the sisters of Henry's father. On the occasions when Henry would return home from college, he would occupy a second floor room in this house.

After graduating from Harvard, Thoreau was invited by Ralph Waldo Emerson and his wife, Lydian, to consider the possibility of moving in with their family. Emerson's far-ranging lecture tour schedule was taking him out of town for long periods of time, and it left his family in

Emerson's "Bush" in Concord, MA

need of an all-purpose handy-man, an expert gardener, and a helper who could both teach and be a companion for the Emerson children. Henry was happy—even honored—to be given the opportunity to provide these services. After all, it had been Emerson whose book *Nature* had inspired the then undergraduate Henry to set his course in life. And it had also been Emerson who had encouraged the young man to write. So, from 1841-1843, Thoreau's Concord residence became the Emerson's "Bush."

There was, however, an important and profound difference between these two men's approach to life. Emerson was a philosopher, an intellectual. He thought deeply and expansively, and assured his many readers and listeners of the worth of their own thoughts and individual revelations. Thoreau's approach to learning and insight was more inwardly directed and more immediately tangible, more rooted in physical reality. In *Walden*, he would write:

> *I went to the woods because I wished to live deliberately, to [con]front only the essential facts of life, and see if I could not learn what it had to teach, and not, when I came to die, discover that I had not lived.* (61)

It would be this desire, expressed with precisely this level of dedication and authenticity, that would ultimately lead Thoreau away, temporarily at least, from the Emerson home. He wanted to experience life in a cabin of his own making on forested land near Concord's most beautiful lake. For Henry David Thoreau the time he spent living by Walden Pond became the turning point of his life.

The Walden Years (1845-1847) and The Dipper

In *Nature*, Emerson had written, "The foregoing generations beheld God and nature face to face, we, through their eyes…Let us demand our own works and laws and worship" (3). Thoreau's response to this observation and challenge sounds very similar to what his mentor had written:

> Next to us the grandest laws are continually being executed. Next to us is not the workman whom we have hired, with whom we love so well to talk, but the workman whose work we are. (Walden 90)

Both men thus acknowledged their need for a new and immediate relationship to Truth, to the Divine force that had planned and created the universe. And furthermore, both implied that this divine presence was nearby, close at hand for anyone willing to recognize and reach out for it.

For Emerson, however, finding this ultimate Truth was a philosophical quest, a matter of intellect, contemplation, and discourse. For Thoreau, finding Truth was a more tactile affair. It was a matter requiring intense and tireless observation of the patterns of the visible world, and the tools he would use to enable him to discover it were boards, nails, an ample supply of firewood, and an indefatigable interest in the minutia of his natural surroundings.

Thoreau's Cabin (replica) near Walden Pond

The book he came to write as the result of his two years living near the shore of Walden Pond would be his masterpiece. It was an instruction manual, a prose poem, an honest account of his failures to find answers to his deepest questions, and finally, a glorious account of his discovery of a key to understanding and appreciating the essential design of all of Nature's vast array of life.

He began *Walden* simply enough, stating that "I should not obtrude my affairs so much on the notice of my readers if very particular inquiries had not been made by my townsmen concerning my mode of life..." (1). Throughout the first two chapters of his work, Thoreau itemized the various decisions and considerations he had to make preparatory to his final move into his one room dwelling on the shores of Walden Pond. In short, he both posed and answered the questions of what is essential for life. And his conclusions were simple and straightforward: food, clothing, shelter, and fuel. Then, in his chapter entitled "Visitors," he made the observation that has given me the title to this chapter: "Many a traveller came out of his way to see me and the inside of my house, and, as an excuse for calling, asked for a glass of water. I told them that I drank at the pond, and pointed thither, offering to lend them a dipper" (101).

From the very outset, Thoreau understood that his decision to establish a small dwelling in the woods would raise questions in the minds of the people who knew him. He was perfectly willing to make an attempt to address their concerns and inquiries. But he also knew that neither he nor his small home would provide them with an understanding of his larger purpose for being there. The land on which he built and the dwelling he had constructed were only perches from which he was initiating his inquiries into the larger issues of life previously mentioned: what is essential, what defines an individual's purpose, what is Truth, and what is the ultimate relationship of Nature itself to these questions. Rather than focusing either on himself or on his tiny residence, Thoreau reminded his visitors that he "drank at the pond, and pointed thither." It was Nature that had led him to this place, and it was in the richness of that same Nature that he hoped to find the answers to his questions.

In this spirit, he offered his visitors "a dipper," a means by which they themselves could drink as he did and thus partake of the quest around which he had founded his life. At first this object was manifested physically, as the metal dipper he himself used to drink from the pond, an item which he was always happy to share with anyone coming out to see him and the one room home he had built. His greater gift, however, would be the "dipper" he would provide for his readers to use in perpetuity to aid them in their own individual attempts to quench their thirst for the larger Truth of the meaning of life itself. This "dipper" would be the book that would result from his sojourn here.

For Thoreau, of course, the stakes were very high. It is important to remember the raw fortitude of his statement in his chapter entitled "Where I Lived and What I Lived for":

> *I wanted to live deep and suck out all the marrow of life, to live so sturdily and Spartan-like as to put to rout all that was not life, to cut a broad swath and shave close, to drive life into a corner, and reduce it to its lowest terms, and, if it proved to be mean, why then to get the whole and genuine meanness of it, and publish its meanness to the world; or if it were sublime, to know it by experience, and be able to give a true account of it in my next excursion.* (61)

Thoreau's "next excursion" would be the writing of *Walden*, and his announced intent, as stated above, was nothing less than discerning the very nature and essence of life itself. Would he find this nature and essence to be "mean" or "sublime"? "I'll tell you when I know the answer," Thoreau seems to state, "and I will tell you the truth, whatever I find." But what if he were to find nothing at all? Would his "account" be just another failure, a list of futile efforts and unanswered questions?

At first, this larger Truth which Thoreau sought continually eluded him. In chapter after chapter, Thoreau's observations, while providing an honest account of his experiences and activities, failed to reveal any of the deeper meanings for which he was searching. Yet he continued to write, undeterred by his missteps. This willingness to chart and map his false starts, his intellectual outtakes, as it were, most clearly exemplifies the moral courage lying at the heart of this remarkable book.

"Brute Neighbors"

No chapter in *Walden* better illustrates Thoreau's willingness to delineate his frustrations than "Brute Neighbors." In and of itself, it is a road map to nowhere, an uncompromising look at a dozen dead ends in Thoreau's search for Truth. Yet within its imagery and structure, the search remains tireless and persistent. Thoreau never doubts that the essence, the "marrow of life" for which he is seeking, is there to be seen, to be felt, to be understood. But he is also having to face the fact that this "marrow" may elude him, that he may not have the stamina, the insight, or even the simple luck to find the answers for which he is seeking.

"Brute Neighbors" chronicles both the emotional cost and the tantalizing possibilities of the search.

The chapter begins with a dialog in which Thoreau's contemplative privacy (he identifies himself as "the Hermit") is interrupted by a poet friend. The poet needs help in order to be able to fish effectively. By the time both men have baited their hooks, Thoreau has lost the train of thought he had been pursuing prior to his friend's intrusion:

> *I was as near being resolved into the essence of things as ever I was in my life. I fear my thoughts will not come back to me. If it would do any good, I would whistle for them. When they make us an offer, is it wise to say, We will think of it? My thoughts have left no track, and I cannot find the path again. (149)*

Whatever his feelings of affection for his poet friend, the invasion of Thoreau's solitude has cost him his inspiration, at least for the present. Perhaps the insight he had experienced was inconsequential, perhaps not. Now he will never know.

As he always does at such moments, Thoreau turns back to nature. His entire experiment at Walden Pond was predicated on the simple, yet profound, assumption that Nature contains the true meaning of life, and, furthermore, that it will willingly communicate this meaning to someone patient enough to hear and see its message.

At this moment in the chapter, Thoreau restates interrogatively his basic credo:

> *Why do precisely these objects which we behold make a world? Why has man just these species of animals for his neighbors...I suspect...they are all beasts of burden, in a sense, made to carry some portion of our thoughts. (150)*

In the absence of revealed truth, Thoreau proceeds to look carefully at the nature that surrounds him and makes vigorous efforts to understand why the nature he perceives constitutes his world. His "Brute Neighbors" become the focus of his attempt to comprehend the larger question that has prompted his entire book: what is the meaning of life?

Thoreau goes on to catalog the various animals he encounters. Each shows itself to be remarkable, extraordinary in some key way. The mice that share his cabin "...were not the common ones," Thoreau notes, and then he proceeds to enumerate their extraordinary habits of running up his clothes, going even so far as to share with him his frugal meals (150). Later, Thoreau describes a partridge "which is so shy a bird" and yet which happily leads "...her brood past my windows" and allows the Hermit to hold one of its young in his hands (151). Perhaps because of their unexpected behavior, Thoreau quickly invests these birds with a significance far beyond their usual category in nature:

> *All intelligence seems reflected in them [the partridges]. They suggest not merely the purity of infancy, but a wisdom clarified by experience.* (151)

The key word in this description is "suggest." Suggestion exists only in the eye of the beholder. Here Thoreau is making nature, in this case the partridges, "carry some portion of [his] thoughts," but the "intelligence," "purity," and "wisdom" he senses in these birds is a suggestion only, a wisdom still written in a hieroglyphic code for which he has yet to find a Rosetta Stone.

Thoreau then goes on to record encounters with four-foot long otters, raccoons, and woodcocks, yet each of these "neighbors" is exceptional only in their willingness to get ever closer to him. This proximity is their allure. Nature is so near, the sought-for Truth seemingly almost within reach, yet its encrypted message continues to daunt Thoreau's best efforts to grasp its ultimate meaning.

Nowhere in this chapter is the majesty and consequence of nature more apparent than in Thoreau's description of ant-warfare. In three long paragraphs ranging over more than two pages, he observes a ferocious battle between red and black ants and finds himself inclined to compare it to other notable human wars:

> *For numbers and for carnage it was an Austerlitz or Dresden. Concord Fight! Two killed on the patriots' side, and Luther Blanchard wounded! Why here every ant was a Buttrick--"Fire! for God's sake fire!"--and thousands shared the fate of Davis and Hosmer. (153)*

While some critics find such comparisons "a parody of historical documentation," it is also possible to sense a much more serious strain within Thoreau's language (Brenner 19). What if, as critic Frederick Garber suggests, "Nature," for Thoreau and all the Transcendentalists, is "emblematic of human possibilities" (130)? Remembering Thoreau's earlier observation that all species are "made to carry some portion of our thoughts," it is hard to resist the conclusion that Thoreau might have seen in the courageous tenacity of the battling ants a parallel to his own tenacious pursuit of natural Truth. Yet the ant battle, as Thoreau's own philosophical struggle, remained indecisive. "I never learned which party was victorious" (154).

And soon thereafter, we encounter the loon. It is fascinating that one of the greatest American poets quickly identified both the beauty and the poetry of Thoreau's account:

> *I'm glad of all the unversified poetry of Walden—and not merely the nature-descriptive, but narrative as in the*

chapter on the play with the loon on the lake...(Robert Frost 8)

The "unversified poetry" to which Frost refers features Thoreau's creation of "a metaphor for man's attempt to lay hold on the mystery of divinity" (Brenner 20). In short, Thoreau concludes his chapter with a recapitulative symbol of the frustrations he has been experiencing in his futile pursuit of the meaning of life. Time and again Thoreau tries to meet–perhaps even catch–the loon, to anticipate precisely where it will surface next. Yet the bird remains both tantalizingly near and completely elusive: "...when I was straining my eyes over the surface [of the pond] one way, I would suddenly be startled by his unearthly laugh behind me" (157). Thoreau finally is left with the only reasonable conclusion: "...he laughed in derision of my efforts, confident of his own resources" (157). It is, after all, men who search for Truth; Truth need not search beyond itself.

In "Brute Neighbors" Thoreau fails to find the pattern, the design of life which he seeks so religiously. Yet his failure is hardly a defeat. Like so much else in *Walden*, both the forthrightness of his quest and the careful observations he has recorded carry a worth of their own. Truth may have eluded Thoreau this time, but the chapter remains resplendent with observations that are both accurate and true. The loon will rise again somewhere, at some time. Thoreau need only wait for it. And continue to write.

The Rosetta Stone

Thoreau spent two years observing and recording his findings in voluminous journal entries. When he came to produce *Walden*, he structured its text in the form of an account of the passing of the four seasons: Summer, Autumn, Winter, and Spring. And it is in the Spring, that season of reawakening and new beginnings, that Thoreau makes his greatest discovery: the very blueprint of all life.

He found it in the most unexpected place imaginable: the railroad cut of the newly laid tracks near the southern edge of the pond.

> *Few phenomena gave me more delight than to observe the forms which thawing sand and clay assume in flowing down the sides of a deep cut on the railroad through which I passed on my way to the village...As it flows it takes the forms of sappy leaves or vines...I am affected as if in a peculiar sense I stood in the laboratory of the Artist who made the world and me—had come to where he was still at work, sporting on this bank, and with excess of energy strewing his fresh designs about. (201, 202)*

Here in this cut of the railroad bed, Thoreau finally discovered the Rosetta Stone of all life, the key to the Truth for which he had been searching so ardently. The "thawing sand and clay" etched a pattern of leaves against the snow, and it was this pattern, Thoreau realized, that was the very blueprint of life itself: of leaves, of course, but also of feathers, bird wings, ice crystals, trees, human veins, and rivers. All living things, it appeared to him, were profoundly unified by this pattern. He rapturously concluded, "Thus it seemed that this one hillside illustrated the principle of all the operations of Nature. The Maker of this earth but patented a leaf" (203).

Yet even this revelation, this discovery, did not in itself fully explain the ultimate meaning of life. It was, like the Rosetta Stone discovered in Egypt by Napoleonic soldiers in 1799, a key to be used to unlock messages hidden in plain sight, either of previously indecipherable hieroglyphs or, in Thoreau's case, of the cycles and infinite variety of the natural world.

Archeologists and scholars studying the Rosetta Stone worked for more than twenty years before they succeeded in being able to use it to translate the ancient Egyptian pictographs reliably. Thoreau understood all too well that the blueprint he had discovered might take just as long or even longer to explicate the full meaning of Nature and of man's place within it. He left his home near Walden Pond after his two-year sojourn there without having found all the answers to the questions that had led him to that place. But he had a clear sense that his discovery, like the Rosetta Stone, might someday lead seekers of Truth to a fuller understanding of "the poem of creation" which the "morning wind forever blows..." (57).

Walden Pond in Concord, MA

I have traveled to Concord several times over the years and have always included a visit to Walden Pond when I did so. I have visited in the early morning hours, at midday, and at dusk, in both summer and spring. I have circumnavigated the pond's thickly forested hillsides in both clockwise and counterclockwise directions, and the experience of doing so has always been quietly and thoughtfully instructive. I have witnessed changes to the pond, varying water levels and an ever-increasing length of sandy shoreline for visitors' and vacationers' enjoyment. My latest visit dates from a late afternoon in August of 2016, and I include an account of it as what I hope will be a satisfying conclusion to this chapter.

"I remember birdsong"

As I made my way down the long ramp from the crowded parking lot area toward the eastern shore of Walden Pond, I found myself thinking back to the words of my longtime friend and professional colleague, Paul O. Williams. He had lamented the addition of a beach and bath house on the shoreline of Walden: "They're turning Walden into a vacation spot instead of preserving the serene beauty Thoreau loved."

When Paul had first made this comment to me, I had not yet had the chance to visit the pond, but I sympathized with and shared his displeasure. Years later, when I finally made it to Concord and was walking around Walden on a cool day in spring, I wondered whether or not Paul might have overreacted. Yes, I noted the bath house and the sandy beach and designated swimming area on the eastern shore of the pond. Obviously, developers had dedicated some space to swimmers and vacationers. But surely, I thought, there are more trees encircling the pond now than there were in Thoreau's day, when almost the entirety of the south bank had been clear cut to accommodate the newly constructed railroad tracks leading into Boston.

And by the time I had made my way down to the site of Thoreau's cabin, I felt a solitude and peace which could only be described as "Thoreauvian." Paul, I concluded, may have been mistaken.

But on this summer day in 2016, it was different.

The sandy beach before the bath house had been extended far beyond the area designated for swimmers. Picnickers had set up coolers, blankets, and umbrellas on the nearby shore. As I began my walk in the woods around the pond, I noted that every path leading down to the water was occupied by rambunctious swimmers, loudly cavorting with their friends in the late afternoon. Their voices carried up the steep banks of the wooded hillsides and echoed loudly across the crystalline waters of the pond as they laughed with and jostled each other.

When I finally arrived at the cabin site on the western end of the pond, I wrote in my journal, "I remember birdsong here—and deep silence, punctuated only by cicadas perhaps or wind sighs in the trees." Not so today, as a family marched up to the cabin site with parents who instructed their children to place a stone on the cairn nearby. "Now can we go back to get in the water?!" their youngest child asked. They all left without further comment.

A couple of minutes later two bicyclists rode up the incline toward the cabin site, dismounting on a steep section of the well-worn path. But they weren't stopping. As they reached the top of the rise, they gave each other a few words of encouragement and prodding, then they remounted and speedily headed off.

From across the water I heard a man with a booming voice cursing at a friend who had forgotten to bring the right brand of beer.

And now, more than ever, I felt that Paul may have gotten it right after all. The spirit of Walden seemed almost irretrievably distant, lost in the clutter of summertime recreation, even as I sat in the middle of the cabin site where Thoreau had lived for two years, searching for Truth.

I was jarred out of my thoughts by the arrival of two young women, one of whom was carrying a large backpack. She wandered up the trail, settled herself on the ground near the cairn adjacent to the cabin site, and swung her pack heavily down beside her. Her friend had stopped to read a placard posted before the spot where the original cabin door had been. It explained, or tried to explain briefly, Thoreau's reasons for settling here.

I suddenly felt as if I was preventing these two new visitors from experiencing the site fully, so I rose up quickly and asked them, "Would you both like to step into the space Thoreau's cabin occupied? I'd be happy to get out of your way." I moved to the side of the area, preparing to leave the site.

"Oh no," the first woman answered me as she rose to join her friend, "but thank you for asking."

"I just don't want to hog it for myself," I added.

Both women laughed and the first woman, an African American with a stunning crown of black hair, noted, "It looks like you're doing what you came here to do." Both she and her friend spoke together quietly, and then the African American woman entered the cabin space and stretched her hand out to me.

"Hello," she began. "I'm Lioness, and this is my friend Val. We were college friends who both read *Walden*, and we thought it would be good to see it together some day, so here we are. What's led you to this place?" she asked me.

"Thirty-seven years of teaching English," I answered her, "and my name is Clark."

"So, you really understand *Walden*?" she asked.

"I taught it before I had seen just how wonderful it was. But I've learned to appreciate what Thoreau was looking for. How about you? Do you love that book?"

Lioness smiled at me and then hurried over to her backpack. "I never stop reading it," she answered me quickly. "I have it right here."

She pulled out of her backpack the most dog-eared copy of *Walden* I have ever seen, and opened it to read to me. "I went to the woods ..."

"...to live deliberately," I finished, and then added "...and not when I came to die..."

"...discover that I had not lived," she concluded softly, after which we both smiled.

Lioness turned page after page, reading aloud quotes that had inspired her. Finally she paused and told me that this was why she had wanted to bring her friend to this place. "I don't think she's understood just how amazingly profound this book is, and I hoped that a visit here would encourage her to look back into it. What more have *you* learned about *Walden*," she asked and then called to her friend, "Come over here, Val. Here's a kindred spirit."

We all talked together for about fifteen minutes. I told them about the dipper and the pattern of the leaves. They shared with me some of their insights and inspirations. And then I noticed that the sun was setting and dusk just beginning to come on.

"My wife, Carol, is waiting for me on the eastern shore, and she's probably wondering what's taking me so long," I told them. "I probably better be going."

Both Lioness and Val understood, and shook hands with me. I left them talking together and reading aloud at the cabin site as I retraced my way back through the wooded edge of the pond.

By this time many of the vacationers had left, at least the most boisterous of them, and I started to hear the susurrus of the wind passing through the leaves. Then, wonderfully enough and for the first time this visit, even the birdsong of a distant mourning dove.

"Paul would have loved that meeting with those two," I found myself thinking. Right there, right amid the idle chatter of a hundred vacationers, was a young woman who revered the man who had lived on the shore of Walden Pond pursuing Truth. She had brought a friend to this place, hoping that it would inspire her to look more deeply into a book they had both read in earlier years. And that book, like the dipper it was, had continued to refresh and challenge her.

Like the leaves fluttering above me, *Walden* was continuing to send out stems to readers and thinkers. It had even warmed the heart of this retired teacher with the hope that Thoreau's insights had not been lost to a new generation. Birdsong indeed to my ears.

5

Bronson and Louisa May Alcott

The Second Floor Foundation

The Alcott's "Orchard House" in Concord, MA

Twelve-year-old Anna Alcott, Louisa May Alcott's elder sister, kept a diary in 1843 in which she described the new living quarters of her family, a communal setting about 15 miles west of Concord, Massachusetts. The small group of idealistic and hopeful settlers of the site had christened their "New Eden" with the name "Fruitlands."

Anna wrote, "It is a beautiful place surrounded by hills, green fields, and woods…There are many pleasant walks about Fruitlands, and berry fields, though the berries are not quite ripe" (*Bronson Alcott's Fruitlands* 100). There is no record of Anna ever speaking cynically, and certainly she was no subtle symbolist, so she probably missed the implicit irony of her concluding comment.

Her younger sister, Louisa May, did not. She put the matter more bluntly. Describing both her father's lofty hopes for Fruitlands as well as his disappointment over its ultimate demise, she recalled its prospectus and recorded its obituary:

> [Father (Bronson)] with the devoutest faith in the high ideal which was to him a living truth, desired to plant a Paradise, where Beauty, Virtue, Justice, and Love might live happily together, without the possibility of a serpent entering in. . . . but it was a failure. The world was not ready for Utopia yet, and those who attempted to found it only got laughed at for their pains…To live for one's principles, at all costs, is a dangerous speculation…. (L.M. Alcott, Transcendental Wild Oats 150, 169)

Today the Fruitlands site is most capably maintained and curated by the Fruitlands Museums, but the pristine and cozy farmhouse visitors see today is a far cry from the relatively dilapidated structure that had awaited the Alcotts, together with the other members of their newly established "consociate family," in June of

1843. Louisa would later describe these utopian idealists as "inspired lunatics, who preached peace on earth and good-will to man so earnestly, with empty pockets" (165). And thus, this experiment in ideal communal living had begun.

"Fruitlands" in Harvard, MA

The central farmhouse provided living space for all the community members. Aside from the individual rooms, there was a kitchen and dining area with a large fireplace. However, the rules of this newly formed Utopian community forbade the eating of "animal substance," including beef, pork, chicken, fish, butter, cheese, eggs, and milk. As a result, hunger soon became the norm at Fruitlands. Even using leather for shoes was frowned upon and discouraged.

There was also a room here at Fruitlands that had been set aside as a library. Brooded over by a bust of Socrates, this setting quickly became Louisa's favorite spot in the house. Here were to be found an ample supply of volumes which offered both enlightenment and solace for the young girl, as well as a reprieve from the arduous labor required simply to keep body and soul together.

Louisa and her sister Anna occupied an attic room on the third floor. Blisteringly hot in summer (it still is) and bitterly cold in winter, its largely unfinished expanse constituted the girls' sole oasis of privacy and peace. While the good weather held, Louisa also enjoyed the open hillside above the farmhouse as a place to ramble after her schooling and chores. Here she could enjoy the expansive view of the valley below her and the thin blue-gray line of mountains on the far horizon to the west.

But by the winter of 1843 the "empty pockets" had yielded their inevitable result. Even with constantly tended fireplaces, the farmhouse had scarcely enough heat to keep the families from freezing.

Ultimately, the Spartan fare, meager crops, and inadequate clothing made life here intolerable. Bronson, the magnetic conversationalist and inspired idealist, fell dangerously ill, took to his bed, turned his face to the wall, and seemed to welcome death.

And then a miracle occurred. Louisa would later recall it in her brief memoir of her half-year spent at Fruitlands:

> *Head had bowed to defeat, hand had grown weary with too heavy tasks, but heart could not grow cold to those who lived in its tender depths, even when death touched it.*
> *"My faithful wife, my little girls, --they have not forsaken me, they are mine by ties that none can break. What right have I to leave them alone? What right to escape from the burden and the sorrow I have helped to bring? This duty remains to me, and I must do it manfully. For their sakes, the world will forgive me in time; for their sakes, God will sustain me now." (171)*

Bronson began eating again, and, as he regained his strength, he determined to bring his precious family back from the brink of destitution and despair to which he had, however unintentionally, led them. The family returned to Concord.

The next four years would be a period of economizing and transplanting themselves, first in Concord and then farther afield. With a gift of $500 from their longtime friend, Ralph Waldo Emerson, the Alcotts were able to buy a house on the Lexington Road which they named "Hillside." The family managed to remain here for three and a half years, the longest time all four of the Alcott daughters would ever spend in one place. Louisa would later revisit her memories of this period in her life as she wrote what would become her most famous novel, Little Women. That, however, was still nearly two decades in the future.

By 1848 the Alcotts' financial situation had once again become critical, and they were forced to sell Hillside and move to Boston. Here, they hoped, work would be more plentiful, and they could pool their resources, saving for happier times.

But they missed the luxury of a permanent home. It would take nearly a decade before the family would return to Concord and purchase "Orchard House," the setting where they would finally be able to put down roots. Yet even when they were on the eve of achieving that goal, the Alcotts would experience a moment of devastating tragedy. While their new home was being refurbished prior to their moving in, their daughter Elizabeth died after a prolonged battle with scarlet fever.

The Alcotts would take possession of Orchard House as a family of five, not six. Yet in this home another one of their daughters, Louisa May, would ultimately join the ranks of the nation's most popular authors. Her literary labors at Orchard House would finally enable her to provide the family with the ongoing and reliable financial security that had always eluded Bronson. In doing so, Louisa May Alcott would also provide her country with one of its most beloved fictional families: the Marches of Little Women.

Bronson would spend the remaining years of his life philosophizing in Concord and traveling throughout the country, holding his famous "conversations" with anyone who offered him a willing ear and a modest remuneration for his company. Indeed, his recorded thoughts on conversation still suggest the almost magical appeal he exerted as a speaker and thinker:

> *All men talk, few converse; of gossip we have enough, of argument more than enough, rhetoric, debate—omit*

these, speak from the heart to the heart underlying all differences, and we have conversation. (Bronson Alcott, *Tablets* 76)

Today's Orchard House is lovingly maintained and staffed by the Louisa May Alcott Memorial Association, and it is as close to a literary holy site as any locale in the United States. As an English teacher for over forty years, I must confess that the reverence brought to this place by its many visitors is a heartwarming reminder of the power and longevity of writing that honestly and tenderly presents the lives and aspirations of its characters. Tourists who stop here to pay homage to Louisa May Alcott's books seem to know the March girls as if they were their own beloved relatives. And this home is curated and presented to its guests in a way that renders it a perfect setting for any expectations they may have brought with them.

But the Orchard House of today would have been almost unrecognizable to the Alcott family who purchased it in 1857. That structure was in such disrepair that it was considered to be virtually valueless. The $975.00 which the Alcotts had paid for the property ($500.00 of which had, once again, been provided by Emerson) was the cost of the twelve-acre piece of land, including an apple orchard on its eastern side. The house had been thrown in gratis. Yet despite its need of significant renovation, Orchard House became a most welcome haven for the Alcotts. It was theirs alone. It was close to Concord and to their many friends. And, most importantly, there would be no more frequent uprootings due to financial insecurity. The family would continue to live here for nearly twenty years.

Although Carol and I had already visited this location, I thought it important to come here again before attempting to write about it. Doing so was an excellent decision. We arrived in Concord early in the day and made our way immediately to Orchard House. After purchasing our tickets, we were invited to join several other visitors who had already gathered in a small side room to see a short film before entering the home proper. The introduction this film provided to the Alcott family and to Orchard House was both informative and interesting. It identified which Alcott related to which member of the March family in *Little Women* [Bronson's "faithful wife," Abigail (or Abba as he called her) = Marmee, Anna = Meg, Louisa May = Jo, Beth = Beth, May = Amy]. We also learned that Bronson Alcott's educational ideas were presented in the book by the character of Professor Bhaer. The film then identified the two most significant family events that had taken place here: Anna's wedding in 1860, and, eight years later in 1868, Louisa May's writing of *Little Women* in her second story room at a semicircular desk placed near one of the front windows. About 85% of the articles on display throughout the house were owned by the Alcotts, the film assured us.

Lastly, it recounted Bronson's building of the hillside chapel nearby in 1880 where he had held meetings of his Concord School of Philosophy in the final years of his life.

As the film ended, our docent, a most engaging and articulate woman whom I will call Rachel, opened a door at the end of the room, and we were shepherded into the kitchen of Orchard House.

Our group stepped into this small space, and, in doing so, several of us noted the floorboards bending slightly under our weight. "A bit rocky," one of us commented. Rachel was quick to notice this and explained, "The floor is old, but sturdy now. When the Louisa May Alcott Memorial Association originally took over the home, they discovered that the house lacked a foundation. They added the necessary structural support to the old fieldstone base, and now the house is more stable than it was when the Alcott family lived here."

Rachel went on to call our attention to the soapstone sink in the room, a luxury that had been provided by Louisa May from money she had earned from her early "somewhat lurid" magazine stories. Rachel also pulled up a square wooden covering over a hole near an outside wall of the kitchen. "This was a well where the family could draw fresh water without leaving the house." It was a helpful reminder not to take for granted the commonplace "luxuries" we all expect to find in our homes: running water, inside toilets, refrigerators, and gas or electric stoves. At least the Alcotts had had water available to them without needing to brave the elements.

"Let's step into the dining room," Rachel continued, opening another door that led further into the interior of the house.

This space was a large rectangular area with a table set for the family. And here also could be seen the first of several examples of May Alcott's paintings that would be in evidence throughout the house. On one wall hung a still life that "had been accepted by the French salon," Rachel informed us. On another wall a rather stern looking portrait of Louisa May was displayed. Rachel noted that Louisa had requested, however comically, that the family should "hang it on the back of the door." Nevertheless, this work was now placed in a spot of honor to recall the memory of the elder sister who had brought the entire family into international prominence through her writing.

"Our next stop is the parlor," Rachel noted and pointed the way for us. "This was the setting of a very important moment for the Alcotts."

The dining room gave directly onto the home's front parlor through an open entry way about six or seven feet wide between partition walls on either side that helped define and separate the two rooms. As we moved into the parlor, light streamed in through the windows on the front of the house. This was a spacious and cheerful room, and Rachel immediately launched into an explanation of the happy event that had transpired here.

"This was the room in which on May 23, 1860, Anna Alcott married John Bridge Pratt. The ceremony was conducted by Abigail's brother, Sam May, a minister, and was attended both by family members and by their dear and longtime friend, Ralph Waldo Emerson."

"This was also the setting," Rachel continued, "of the theatricals the girls used to love to present. They would hang a curtain over the entryway to the dining room, and spectators would sit in the parlor. When the curtain was drawn the dining room area became the girls' stage. And here," Rachel led our gazes over to a table on which several ribbons were laid out, "are the actual headbands the girls wore, identifying them as members of their troupe, the Pickwick Club."

As I stood near the table on which these faded, delicate, but carefully preserved ribbons were laid out, I felt the world of Louisa May and her sisters come vividly to life before me. "As the oldest," Rachel informed us, "Anna's ribbon bore the name 'Pickwick.' Sister Beth had been 'Tupman.' The last of these ribbons, marked only 'P.C.,' belonged either to Louisa May whose *Pickwick Papers* character was Augustus Snodgrass or to her little sister, May, who chose Nathaniel Winkle as her character." The world of the Alcott girls seemed almost tangible here. One could easily imagine the giggles from behind the curtained off dining room as the thespians prepared their parts. The audience's fond anticipation. The exaggerated articulation of the actors. It was all very real.

Our docent let us all have a moment to look at these precious artifacts, and then she continued our tour. "Now let's go upstairs to the bedrooms. The piano near the stairway is a reminder of Beth's love of that instrument." We all ascended the creaky wooden stairs quietly and found ourselves in a hallway leading to several separate rooms. Our very first stop was Louisa May's bedroom which included her study and writing space.

It also, Rachel informed us, had been her sick room at a critical moment of her life. In 1862 it had been Louisa, and not the father described in her great novel, who had gone to war. She had served as a nurse in a military hospital in Georgetown. After a month and a half, Louisa had become so severely ill that she was forced to leave her hospital duties. She returned home to Concord, to this very room, and, with the tireless aid of her family, had slowly begun to recover—though her health was never again to approach the strength of her earlier years. Her artist sister, May, had placed in her room the likenesses of two owls, one a sculpture and the other an oil painting which hung over the bed. Had Louisa always regarded these birds as her personal favorites? Were these images to be seen as May's acknowledgment of the wisdom and insight of this other "artist" in the Alcott family? None of us thought to pose such questions as our docent diverted our attention to the room's most important literary feature.

In 1868, six years after her recovery, Louisa would sit at the semi-circular desk in this room, a writing desk her father had fashioned especially for her, and, however hesitantly at first, would turn her attention to the life she and her sisters had lived years earlier at Hillside. Abandoning the dark and sensational fiction she had written in earlier years, Louisa now recorded memories of her sisters and parents, of Concord life, and of a world of selfless poverty, enduring love, agonizing loss, surprising happiness, and heroic perseverance, all of which she had experienced firsthand. Her publisher, rather than she, had suggested a name for her novel: *Little Women*. And here it was before us—the very heart of Orchard House.

There were other rooms to see on this level, of course. Rachel led us next to May's long arched room next door, with a striking blue stripe painted where the walls met the ceiling. Of particular note here, aside from the arched ceiling which, Rachel informed us, had both accommodated May's height and pleased her aesthetic sensibilities, were actual preserved drawings on the walls. The Alcotts had encouraged their youngest child to use her room as a canvas on which to hone her craft, and remarkably, several of these drawings, on both the front wall beneath her window and on her cupboard door, had been preserved.

Across the hall was Bronson's and Abigail's room. It was a sunny and serviceable master bedroom with windows on both the front and side walls. Once again, as had been the case throughout the rest of the house, May's art was on prominent display here.

Rachel then led us back downstairs to the final stop of our tour: Bronson's library and study. Located directly beneath his and Abigail's bedchamber, it too featured windows on two walls, and shafts of golden light flooded its interior. "Bronson's longtime friend, Ralph Waldo Emerson, would say of this room, 'Here there is always light,' " Rachel reminded us, and it seemed clear that Emerson's statement, as was typical of the great Transcendental philosopher, referred less to the physical illumination of this space than to his friend's great intellectual worth.

As I stood quietly enjoying the unspoken eloquence of this room, the words of another of Bronson's closest friends, Henry David Thoreau, came to my mind:

> *If you have built castles in the air, your work need not be lost; that is where they should be. Now put the foundations under them. (Walden 214)*

If ever a man had "built castles in the air," it had been Bronson Alcott. Philosopher, utopian idealist, incomparable conversationalist, unrepentant dreamer. Bronson had been all these things. They had led him to fruitless Fruitlands. But he had also dearly loved his long-suffering wife and young daughters, and that love had saved him. It had ultimately led them to Orchard House. Yet even this lovely setting had been a home without an adequate foundation. The Alcotts would need Louisa May to provide that.

Using episodes from her own family life years earlier at Hillside, Louisa's fictional March family was grounded in many of her fondest, as well as some of her most vividly devastating, memories. Her portrayal of what she had learned and what she had experienced, neither saccharine sweet nor broodingly melancholic, rang undeniably true for her ever-widening reading audience. Her mother Abigail's selfless labors and quiet wisdom were mirrored in the tireless patience and subtle insights of Marmee. Her elder sister, Anna, and her many lessons as both a young wife and mother, were given new life in the character of Meg. Jo March embodied both the aspirations and the contradictions and self-doubt that Louisa herself knew all too well. And May March, the youngest of the sisters, with her flair for the arts, was a clear and loving portrait of Louisa's younger sister Amy, whose artistic studies still adorn the walls of her bedroom at Orchard House. Beth, dear unassuming Beth, is the only character whose name Louisa never changed. Beth's delicate life and heart-wrenching death were part of the tapestry of *Little Women* that needed no embellishment.

Her novel changed the direction of fiction in America. Bronson's utopian "castles in the air" had remained, to a great degree, ethereal visions. Louisa May's book was more down to earth. And its astonishing success assured a stable financial footing on which the Alcotts would rely for the rest of their lives. The sturdy foundation that Bronson had sought throughout so many years had finally been put in place.

Unlike most foundations, however, this one had never been physically located beneath the house it supported. And the general contractor providing it was a woman whose only tool had been her pen. It had been added to the property from a most unusual location: from a manuscript crafted in a room on the second floor. The stability and legacy of both the Alcotts and Orchard House had come to rest on the bedrock of Louisa May's unique synthesis of remembrance and imagination recorded in the pages of her masterpiece, *Little Women*.

6

Nathaniel Hawthorne

Clytie

The Old Manse in Concord, MA

Attempting to trace the many transplantings of Nathaniel Hawthorne throughout his native state of Massachusetts is a somewhat complicated task. His birthplace in Salem still stands, though moved from its first location, and his lunching spot in the graveyard of King's Chapel near the Custom House in Boston is a tourist stop on that city's famous Freedom Trail. A replica of the Hawthornes' rental cottage in the Berkshires has been placed on its original site, and the Wayside, the only home that Hawthorne ever owned, is part of the Minute Man National Park. But since it was while he was living in the Old Manse in Concord, Massachusetts, that Hawthorne felt his adult life had truly begun, it is there that this chapter opens.

Hawthorne's years living at the Old Manse in Concord were some of the happiest and most productive periods of his life. His second floor study there reveals an essential truth that is reflected in all of his greatest works. Hawthorne's inspiration was rooted in his own rich imagination. External observations of people or places were only of secondary interest to him. Imagination and a passionate love of language formed the basis of his art.

I have visited the Old Manse on four separate occasions over the years, and, upon entering this study, I always get a feeling of being on literary holy ground. In this very room a young Ralph Waldo Emerson had begun the work that would become *Nature* and initiate the first great school of distinctly American philosophic thought, Transcendentalism.

And then, fewer than 10 years later in 1842, Nathaniel Hawthorne had begun his married life with Sophia Peabody as renters of the Old Manse. He claimed this same room as a study in which he would write some of his most popular short stories. Both he and Sophia left their signatures here, in what I have always felt to be the very spirit of young love. On one of the western windows, and looking out toward the gently meandering Concord River, the couple engraved the following sentiments:

> *Man's accidents are God's purposes.*
> *Sophia A. Hawthorne, 1843*
>
> *Nathaniel Hawthorne. This is his study.*
>
> *The smallest twig leans clear against the sky*
> *Composed by my wife and written with her diamond*
>
> *Inscribed by my husband at Sunset April 3, 1843*
> *In the Gold light*
> *SAH*

The sparsely furnished room measures seventeen by twelve feet, and has three outlooks, two western-facing windows and one window facing north, where in Emerson's day, one could still see clearly the site of the Old North Bridge. A small fireplace occupies the center of the eastern wall.

When Emerson wrote here, his desk was positioned near the windows of the room. To the north he could look out at the place where the early colonists had first taken a stand against the British soldiers sent to Concord to disarm the local population. At the western windows, he could gaze out at the ever-changing beauty of Nature, a beauty that he would come to appreciate in spiritual as well as in physical terms.

Hawthorne made a very different choice in establishing his writing place. He commissioned the addition of a small writing surface attached to the eastern wall directly next to the fireplace.

The result was a writing space completely turned away from any of the room's windows. For Hawthorne, clearly, his inspiration came from within. The visible world could only distract him from the rich imaginative landscape which inspired the literature he was so determined to produce.

The Hawthornes lived for three years at the Manse, enjoying a blissfully extended honeymoon. Their first child, Una, was born in the second floor bedroom, and Hawthorne had written prolifically in the study just down the hall. His tales included such masterworks as "Young Goodman Brown," "Rappaccini's Daughter," and "The Celestial Railroad." Soon these stories along with twenty-two others would be published in a two-volume set entitled *Mosses from an Old Manse*. This collection would garner even more critical praise than had his first volume of short stories, *Twice-Told Tales*. But in the autumn of 1845 and at the age of 42, Hawthorne was forced to acknowledge that the financial result of his literary efforts left much to be desired. He had found it impossible to pay his bills. The family had fallen behind in their rent. And suddenly Hawthorne had received notice that, due to his failure to meet these financial obligations, the family was being told to vacate the Manse in order to make room for a new tenant.

With no other acceptable option open before him, Hawthorne decided to move his family to Salem, the town where he had been born. What would the future hold for them? As they quickly packed their belongings for this forced removal, Nathaniel may well have sympathized with Milton's Adam and Eve, expelled from the Eden they had loved:

> They, looking back, all th'Eastern side beheld
> Of Paradise, so late their happy seat,...
> Some natural tears they dropped, but wiped them soon,
> The world was all before them, where to choose
> Their place of rest, and Providence their guide;

> *They hand in hand with wandering steps and slow,*
> *Through Eden took their solitary way.*

Salem, Massachusetts was a far cry from Eden, but, for Nathaniel at least, it had the advantage of being familiar ground. He rented a room on Chestnut Street where the family could live together, albeit in rather crowded conditions. Meanwhile he clung desperately to the hope that perhaps a friend might help him find some sort of gainful employment. By June of the following year, the family's financial needs were suddenly met and from a most unexpected source. Nathaniel Hawthorne had become the beneficiary of the political spoils system.

Hawthorne had been an enthusiastic member of the Democratic party since his Bowdoin College days in Brunswick, Maine. While there he had become a close friend of Franklin Pierce, a fellow undergraduate who, in later years, would be elected both a Democratic Representative, then Senator from his native state of New Hampshire. In November of 1844, Democrat James K. Polk was elected the 11th President of the United States. This turned out to be a most auspicious development for Hawthorne. Through the enthusiastic support of his friends and literary admirers, he found himself being offered the position of Surveyor of the Custom House in Salem, a prestigious political appointment.

The position would provide a reliable and comfortable income. It would also carry along with it an aura of social dignity that the young Hawthorne family had never yet enjoyed. After all, only six years earlier Nathaniel had been employed at the Custom House in Boston as a measurer of salt and coal. Now he would be a central figure in the Salem Custom house, overseeing what was at that time one of the most important ports in the United States. Furthermore, he hoped, this new position might even give him more time and opportunity in the afternoons and evenings to pursue his writing career, unharried by the demands of making ends meet. He gratefully accepted the job, and on the strength of this new appointment, was able to rent a large home on Mall Street.

All the evidence suggests that Hawthorne started upon the duties of his new position fully committed to doing an exemplary job. He appeared to have been a perfect choice for the post. He was intelligent, industrious, and dedicated to the work. He was also extremely grateful for the salary and security this position provided him. And, as he had hoped, his afternoons and evenings were often free. But regardless of all this, he found himself unable to write. It was as if his Muse had deserted him, at least for the moment. The post did not encourage his literary sensibilities. He would later try to explain the difficulties he encountered in this period of his life:

> *Literature, its exertions and objects, were now of little moment in my regard. I cared not, at this period, for books; they were apart from me...A gift, a faculty, if it had not departed, was suspended and inanimate within me...this was a life which could not, with impunity, be lived too long; else, it might make me permanently other than I had been.... (SL 23-24)*

Custom House in Salem, MA

The Salem Custom House still stands near the waterfront as a reminder of the town's rich economic history. A quick visit offered at least a partial explanation of why Hawthorne felt a loss of his imaginative "gift" during his employment here.

After mounting the twelve high white granite stairs leading to the building's main entrance, visitors are regaled with information delivered by friendly and informative park guides. Their remarks are full of detailed accounts of the precision necessary to the successful running of a 19th century Custom House. Guides assure visitors that everything having to do with the essential business transacted here had depended on absolute accuracy in determining and recording facts. What items were being exported or imported? And in what volumes? What were the exact weights of every shipment? What were the precise tariffs or export fees assigned to each item? What, if any, of the imported items would need to be stored in the warehouse behind the Custom House until their assessed fees had been paid in full? Did every approved item carry on it the necessary stenciled name of the Surveyor, "N. Hawthorne"? Nothing could be left to chance nor any cargo remain uninspected. No business transacted here was subject to approximation nor guesswork. Everything on every day was counted, weighed, recorded, and processed precisely according to the established procedure.

After a year or two, Hawthorne would write later, the job had become "a hopeless toil." His final comment about this chapter of his life was brutally frank: "... it is anything but agreeable to be haunted by a suspicion that one's intellect is dwindling away" (34).

Custom House Stairs in Salem, MA

As Carol and I left the Custom House on a late afternoon in August, 2016, I looked down the rather steep stairway leading to the street where our car was parked. Suddenly I was struck with the sight of an elaborate decorative pattern that stretched down the entire length of the right-hand side of the granite steps. "Carol," I called out. "Look at the stairway. It's covered with lines and swirls that I didn't notice when we entered. What an amazing design!"

Carol looked at me and smiled. "You didn't notice them because they weren't there when we entered," she said. "The position of the sun changed while we were touring the Custom House. They are shadows cast by the iron railing. Really beautiful, though."

Of course, she was right, and I was momentarily embarrassed that I hadn't seen the truth more quickly. But I also wondered if these delicate and imaginative tracings on the granite stairs would have been seen by Hawthorne as he headed for home in the late summer afternoons.

"Was this iron railing here when Nathaniel Hawthorne was Surveyor?" I asked the park ranger who was just closing up the building as we had been his last guests.

"Yes, sir," he answered me. "It was here even before his period of service."

Then at least, I thought, there had been something unexpected, something almost magical in this place for Hawthorne to witness. Had he ever stopped to look at these fascinating shadows? And if so, had they seemed to him to be fanciful exceptions to the stern, unchanging regimen of the Custom House? I will never know the answers to such questions, but whether or not Hawthorne had ever stopped to notice them, his world was about to change abruptly.

What the spoils system of American politics had bestowed upon him, it now took away. With the election of the Whig candidate, Zachary Taylor, in 1848, a new administration came into power, and, with it, a new appointee to the position of Surveyor of the Salem Custom House. Suddenly Hawthorne was unemployed. He returned to his rental house on Mall Street with only the money he and Sophia had managed to save during his years as Surveyor to provide for their necessities.

Hawthorne's rental home in Salem, MA

But now almost by some kind of magic, Hawthorne's imaginative powers began to return to him. Whether it was the natural result of his immediate need for an occupation, or simply because of the lessening of the responsibilities of managing the Custom House, Hawthorne's Muse reawakened, none the worse for wear after what had been a forced and regretted suspension. Once again words began to flow. Not short stories any more, but a longer work, cast in a form he would come to term a "Romance."

Recalling his days as a laborer in the Boston Custom House, Hawthorne remembered his frequent lunchtime repasts in the graveyard of King's Chapel on Tremont Street and the crooked grave marker of a woman named Elizabeth Pain that featured a halfway concealed letter A in a coat of arms etched into the stone. Her story, set in 17th century Boston and supposedly also inspired by a long-lost relic Hawthorne claimed to have found in the attic of the Salem Custom House, told the tale of a forbidden love affair, of an intractable and self-destructive revenge, and of an ultimate spiritual victory. It was lengthier and more thoroughly developed than anything he had written before.

At first Hawthorne was uncertain as to whether or not his "Romance" would have any appeal to readers. But James T. Fields, his publisher, had no such doubts. When Fields arrived in Salem to visit with his author/client, Hawthorne gave him a manuscript copy of the new work. Fields was immediately struck with the story, believing that its characters, style, and themes would resonate with a large audience. He enthusiastically approved its publication. This novel, *The Scarlet Letter*, would become the breakthrough for which Hawthorne had been hoping for many years. At last he was about to be more widely known and appreciated as one of his country's most important writers.

But not in Salem. There were questions being raised about his conduct as Surveyor of the Custom House, questions that suggested that his removal from that post might have been occasioned by more than the recent election of a Whig president. And to make matters worse, the introductory chapter of *The Scarlet Letter*, entitled "The Custom House," included rather pointedly satirical portraits of various personages Hawthorne had come to know there, citizens who were widely respected and venerated. By the end of March 1850, the entire family was beginning to feel increasingly unwelcome in Salem.

Despite the initial success of *The Scarlet Letter*, the Hawthornes were more than a little mindful of their still straightened and even somewhat precarious financial state. Realizing that their present means were insufficient to meet the expenses of their Mall Street address, they decided to move west near Lenox, Massachusetts, where they had found a small rental cottage in the Berkshire Hills. Here, Hawthorne looked forward to being able to continue to write in peace. By year's end this new location would also come to offer the added benefit of proximity to the family of a new acquaintance, Herman Melville, a fellow writer who had recently praised Hawthorne's *Mosses from an Old Manse* for its tone and command of language.

At first the move seemed to have been quite profitable. The Hawthornes could easily afford the rent of the small red cottage in the Berkshire Hills. The family enjoyed the quiet remoteness of their new setting, and, happily, by the end of September, the Melvilles had pur-

Hawthorne's Rental Cottage near Lenox, MA

chased property nearby and were both friendly and copacetic neighbors.

Although the original cottage the Hawthornes rented has not survived, a replica has been reconstructed on its original site on the grounds of what is now Tanglewood, a summer venue for the world-famous Boston Symphony. The cottage is currently filled with practice rooms where musicians can rehearse prior to performances. It is not open for visitors, but one can still see the misty mountains in the surrounding landscape. The setting feels isolated, even today in the midst of summer tourist activity.

As Hawthorne settled into his new home, he immediately set about writing another extended tale, this one stemming from his visits to and memories of the oldest home in Salem, the 17th and 18th century home that he would transform through his fiction into one of the country's most famous literary landmarks: The House of the Seven Gables. Interestingly enough, Hawthorne never saw the home in the condition tourists see it in today. The house he knew had been remodeled several times over the years and had only three gables. The property had passed into the hands of his cousin, Susanna Ingersoll, and she often invited Nathaniel to visit and told him tales of the original home built by a sea captain in 1688 who managed during his lifetime to oversee several additions to the original structure and transformed it into seven-gabled splendor. Hawthorne's reawakened imaginative powers had been fired by these visits and constituted some of the most important baggage he had taken along with him as he and his family had moved west.

In his cottage study, Hawthorne restored in his imagination all seven gables that had once been the pride of the sea captain's house in Salem. Then in his fiction he peopled it with characters consumed by greed and haunted by memories

The House of the Seven Gables in Salem, MA

of both an ancient and a modern injustice inflicted on innocent men. The book that resulted, *The House of the Seven Gables*, would sell even more copies than had *The Scarlet Letter*.

Soon Hawthorne would begin a third novel, *The Blithedale Romance*, in which he would once again use his imaginative powers to reconstruct and refashion his memories, this time of his sojourn in the now-defunct "utopia" of Brook Farm. For the first and only time in his fiction, he would include a self-portrait in his cast of characters, as well as a tragically drawn reimaging of an extraordinary woman he had met there: Margaret Fuller.

But despite the cottage's admirable situation for creative work, the family ultimately found life in the Berkshires too isolated and remote, too lonely a place for them to want to remain there indefinitely. They hoped to return to a larger community, though one that would still possess the peace and quiet needed for Nathaniel's writing.

Perhaps because of their happy memories of the years they had spent at the Old Manse, the Hawthornes decided to return to Concord. If they could only find the right property, the growing family might be able to put down roots in a permanent home.

The house they found still stands and sits just off the Lexington Road on the east side of the village of Concord. Finally, they would have a home they could call their own. Interestingly enough, it was a somewhat storied location even before the Hawthornes purchased the property.

Nearly a century earlier, in April of 1775, the house had borne silent witness to British soldiers retreating back to Boston at the end of their disastrous military incursion into nearby Lexington and Concord during which had been fired "the shot heard round the world."

Then late in 1843 the property had been purchased by Bronson Alcott who gave it the name of "Hillside." The Alcotts would live here for only four years, but the period of their residence would be fondly remembered by one of their daughters, Louisa May. "Hillside" would provide the setting for her most beloved novel, *Little Women*.

Hawthorne's "The Wayside" in Concord, MA

Hawthorne purchased the house in 1852 and renamed it "The Wayside," as a more exactly accurate description of its physical location. He began remodeling the house in hopes that it could be turned into a haven where he and his family could happily spend the rest of their lives. How could he know that forces were already at work that would take him away from Concord for the next seven years? And even more significantly, how could he know, as he was putting the finishing touches on *The Blithedale Romance* here at "The Wayside," that his greatest literary successes were now behind him? Nathaniel was about to be lured, once again, away from his imaginative labors and back into the world of politics and the spoils system.

1852, the year of the Hawthorne family's move back to Concord, was also an election year. Nathaniel had just sent off the finished manuscript of The Blithedale Romance to his publisher in Boston when he received a visit at the still being refurbished Wayside from his longtime friend, Franklin Pierce. Would the now-famous author and old Bowdoin college roommate be willing to write a campaign biography that would introduce voters to the character and qualifications of his friend, Pierce, the newly chosen dark horse Democratic candidate for the presidency?

Of course he would. Hawthorne had suggested as much in a letter he had sent to Pierce after learning of his nomination. And so, for the first and only time in American history, a presidential biography was penned by one of America's most admired novelists. When the election results were tallied, Pierce found himself the 14th President of his nation.

Hawthorne, of course, was delighted with his friend's success. The family was even more delighted, however, when the news came that Nathaniel Hawthorne had been chosen by the President to fill the role of U.S. Consul to Liverpool, England, arguably one of the most prestigious political appointments Pierce could have offered his biographer. As Consul, Hawthorne would be representing the maritime interests of the United States with its most important trading partner in the most important port in Great Britain. The salary involved would put to rest any financial concerns the family might have for their foreseeable future. This offer was the Custom House appointment on steroids.

Hawthorne gratefully accepted the appointment and soon thereafter the family left the still uncompleted Wayside and relocated to England. Hawthorne would devote himself to the important diplomatic duties of this new post for the duration of Pierce's presidential term.

At the expiration of his Consular duties with the onset of President James Buchanan's administration, neither Hawthorne nor his family wanted to return immediately to the United States. Now well-off and with time on his hands, he decided to travel in Europe, ultimately spending two additional years there, enjoying its scenery and in particular the beauty and antiquity of Italy. Cloistering himself in a tower study in the Villa Montauto near Florence, he returned to his writing and produced a new Romance, *The Marble Faun*. The initial reviews were generally favorable, largely due to Hawthorne's splendid descriptions of the Italian landscape. But ultimately public interest in the book waned, as its vague and confusing conclusion discouraged and bewildered readers. Hawthorne tried to add a few explanatory pages to subsequent editions of the work, but they failed to alter the verdict his audience had already passed upon it.

The family returned to Concord in 1860, just as the country was spiraling into civil war. At home once again in Wayside, Hawthorne recommenced the architectural additions he had begun seven years earlier. After the family's extended stay in Italy, however, Hawthorne's desires for his home had expanded. Most of all he wanted to recreate the tower study he had enjoyed in the Villa Montauto and, by doing so, insure for himself a workroom where he could continue his writing career.

He was disappointed, however, with the results of his New England workmen. The elegance of Italian Gothic architecture had eluded them, though the finished addition did include a spacious formal parlor on the back of the house and a second floor bedroom for Una, as well as the tower study he had requested.

Trying to make the best of things, Hawthorne climbed up the narrow staircase to the tower and ensconced himself in this new study. Standing at a writing table he had fashioned himself, and with his back turned away from the window as had always been his preference, he attempted to reignite the imagination that had lain largely dormant for the years of his diplomatic service in Europe. To no avail. His Muse had finally deserted him. The warning he had given himself years earlier after his stint at the Salem Custom House now seemed doubly true:

> ...this was a life which could not, with impunity, be lived too long; else, it might make me permanently other than I had been.... (SL 23-24)

Of course, Hawthorne was still regarded as one of the greatest American writers. He had many friends and admirers. Finally abandoning the thought of producing a new Romance, he spent his working hours writing an extended travel narrative recounting his observations of England. And in spite of his publisher's plea not to do so, he dedicated this work, *Our Old Home*, to his longtime friend and patron, Franklin Pierce, the now widely discredited and rejected ex-President. The book sold poorly.

By 1864, with civil war raging throughout the country, Hawthorne had fallen seriously ill. He decided to take a trip to the mountains of New England in hopes of recovering his health there and chose Franklin Pierce as his traveling companion. Pierce readily agreed to accompany him, but Hawthorne's condition worsened quickly. He died of his illness in a New Hampshire hotel with his old friend by his bedside. His body would make one last journey back to Concord and The Wayside, overseen by the 14th President of the United States.

It is tempting to conclude that the interruption of his imaginative genius with the exacting business practices and demands of international economic diplomacy had essentially ended the creative life of the great writer. And there is evidence in the tower room that Hawthorne himself had come to realize this fact rather poignantly. Among the sculpture busts he placed on wall shelves around the room, images of Plato and Ben Franklin, Daniel Webster and the educator Johann Pestalozzi, stands the bust of a minor Greek water nymph, Clytie. Once beloved of the god Apollo, she had betrayed him in a fit of jealousy and thus had completely lost his favor. Clytie spent the rest of her life looking up as Apollo passed through the sky above her, but she never again received from him any of the love, inspiration, or attention for which she so passionately yearned. The presence of her image here suggests that Hawthorne may have understood more fully than most the devastating meaning of that myth.

Yet his greatest works live on. Like the shadowy tracings on the granite steps of the Salem Custom House, Hawthorne's stories and Romances with their evanescent swirls of unexpected and mysterious beauty can continue to fascinate and enthrall any reader who is still willing to lend them the time and thoughtful attention they both require and deserve. In these creations Hawthorne's spirit remains vividly present, his back to the window and his face to the wall, patiently awaiting the arrival of some new imaginative and compelling dream.

7

Emily Dickinson

"She had the world she wanted."

Emily Dickinson's Homestead in Amherst, Massachusetts

I had imagined it differently. Surely, I had thought, it would be more isolated. Perhaps a humble village dwelling with a modestly sized adjacent garden tucked into a corner of a quiet street or settled at the end of an unfrequented country lane. Certainly not this beautiful and spacious home cresting a hillside on the main road of Amherst, just south of the town center. And this was only the first surprise I encountered during Carol's and my visit here in the summer of 2017. It reminded me once again of the importance of visiting the homes and settings where writers have written. These locales inevitably both surprise me and add flavorful new insights to my understanding and appreciation of the writers whose works have led me to these places.

And what an exciting new dimension of Emily Dickinson revealed itself to us as we toured this attractive home. Our docent was a gentleman named Steve (whose closing comment in our tour provides the title to this chapter). He was a marvelous guide through the two properties available for visiting. His words also provided a new and refreshing perspective regarding Dickinson that, time and again, the site confirmed.

"She had the world she wanted," he concluded after leading us through both the Dickinson family home and the nearby Evergreens house, a gift of Dickinson's father to his son and daughter-in-law in 1856. "But how could Steve's conclusion possibly be true?" (I found myself asking, though not aloud.) This was Emily Dickinson, the unhappily withdrawn spinster most of whose poetry had only been published posthumously. Emily Dickinson, whose life was tragically confined and whose soul found relief in poetry as her only solace from the many disappointments that had plagued her all too abbreviated life. After all, wasn't it Dickinson who had written in one of the few poems published during her lifetime:

> Success is counted sweetest
> By those who ne'er succeed.
> To comprehend a nectar
> Requires sorest need.
>
> Not one of all the purple host
> Who took the flag today
> Can tell the definition,
> So clear, of victory,
>
> As he, defeated, dying,
> On whose forbidden ear
> The distant strains of triumph
> Break, agonized and clear.

I had been taught that such words had described, even defined, the life of Emily Dickinson. "Sorest," "defeated," "forbidden," "distant," and "agonized." How could such a life, or such a poet, have had "the world she wanted"? But then I found myself remembering both the homes we had just visited and the facts about Dickinson's life that Steve had shared with us—many of which I had never encountered in my research. They forcibly reminded me of a great truth: no one is one dimensional. And this is particularly true of our greatest artists. Their humanity includes many moods, sometimes even seismic shifts of opinions and perspectives. They experience both joy and sorrow, both doubt and certainty, and yet, perhaps most importantly, they still manage to choose the life they live in ways that others may never fully understand. Hadn't Dickinson also written, I now recalled,

> The soul selects her own society,
> Then shuts the door;
> On her divine majority
> Obtrude no more.

> *Unmoved, she notes the chariot's pausing*
> *At her low gate;*
> *Unmoved, an emperor is kneeling*
> *Upon her mat.*
>
> *I've known her from an ample nation*
> *Choose one;*
> *Then close the valves of her attention*
> *Like stone.*

This is no hymn to victimization, written by a soul forced into solitary confinement. The writer of this poem is in complete control of her life. It is she, *her* soul, that "shuts the door," not her society that has somehow excluded her from its graces. Her "divine majority" is not to be obtruded upon. She notes chariots and emperors, but is "unmoved." It is she who chooses "one" from "an ample nation." It is she who closes "the valves of her attention/ Like stone." This is a poem about independence and independent decision making. A far cry from the helplessness or despair or regretted loneliness that is so often forwarded as the key to understanding the life and works of this great poet.

It is interesting to me that many of Dickinson's most ardent admirers appreciate her life and works largely because they feel themselves to be kindred souls with her, the result of what they perceive to be some shared interest, passion, or cause. Her poetry, however, almost always proves her to be tantalizingly elusive. What is undeniable is that her verses invariably illustrate her passionate dedication to meticulous observation. Also that she was courageously willing to explore, examine, and even accept occasional inconsistencies in her own opinions and states of mind.

Carol's and my visit here to her home in Amherst, Massachusetts, has challenged or at least seriously modified several of the assertions one often finds written about the life of Emily Dickinson. Assertions such as these: 1) She died in the same house in which she had been born; 2) She was obsessed with death; 3) She was an atheist; 4) Her tragic disappointments in love left her bitter and depressed; 5) She was regarded as a "strange woman" by the citizens of Amherst, and no one in town was aware of her habit of writing poetry until her scribbled verses were discovered after her death.

I have found it worthwhile to examine the aforementioned assertions, both in light of her poetry and from the perspective of the information one receives here at the Dickinson home in Amherst. Doing so often qualifies and even occasionally contradicts what is often taught regarding her life and work.

Assertion #1) She died in the same house in which she had been born.

This statement, Steve informed us, while literally true, is still misleading in an important way. It implies that Dickinson had lived in only one home for the entirety of her life, and this is not so. Samuel Fowler Dickinson, Emily's grandfather and a successful lawyer, had built the residence in 1813. His son, Edward, also a lawyer, moved into the western half of the home with his wife and young son Austin in 1830. Emily was born here in December of the same year. In 1833 Samuel sold the home to David Mack, the proprietor of a general store in Amherst, and for six more years the Dickinsons shared the house as a duplex with the Mack family. Emily resided here until she was nine years old, at which time her father had made enough financial progress to buy another house in town on Pleasant Street. Although that home no longer stands, it would be Emily's residence for the next sixteen years.

In 1855 the Mack property again became available. Edward purchased the original family house, and the Dickinson's moved back in, this time occupying it in its entirety. Here Emily would spend the rest of her life. Yet the sixteen years she spent on Pleasant Street would come to have a very significant effect upon her poetry.

Assertion #2) She was obsessed with death.

This assertion would appear to be undeniable. The first lines of several of her most famous poems illustrate vividly this fixation: "Because I could not stop for death," "There's been a death in the opposite house," "I heard a fly buzz when I died," "I felt a funeral in my brain." The list goes on and on. And yet our visit to Amherst cast even this assertion into a new light. Steve reminded us that not only had the family moved to Pleasant Street for sixteen formative years in the life of their daughter, but also that the view from her room in that house looked directly out onto a nearby church's graveyard. "For any child," Steve noted, "such an outlook might be sobering, but for a girl as sensitive as Emily, it can hardly be counted as an obsession that she was constantly reminded of the fact of death. And of course," he continued, "Dickinson *had* experienced several personal losses. Her second cousin, Sophia Holland, her dear friend Benjamin Newton, and a beloved teacher, Leonard Humphrey, all died before Emily had reached her twenty-fourth year. But what is remarkable," Steve continued, "was the extent to which Emily remained fascinated by and minutely observant of life and living things."

Assertion #3) She was an atheist.

This assertion rests almost exclusively on Emily's exit from Mount Holyoke Female Seminary in 1848 as a student placed in the category of "No Hope" because of her refusal to profess her faith to Christ and Christianity. Most modern scholars have forwarded other explanations for her departure from this prestigious school, but regardless of her motivations in this matter Dickinson would also write:

> I never saw a moor,
> I never saw the sea;
> Yet know I how the heather looks,
> And what a wave must be.
>
> I never spoke with God,
> Nor visited in heaven;
> Yet certain am I of the spot
> As if the chart were given.

If nothing else, the sentiment expressed here suggests a formidable level of spiritual certainty. While not doctrinal in any specifically theological sense, it is decidedly not atheistic. The poem speaks for itself.

Assertion #4) Her tragic disappointments in love left her bitter and depressed.

Of all the assertions clustered around the name of Emily Dickinson, this one is the most difficult to untangle. A large part of the difficulty lies in the fact that this is also the area of Dickinson's life that has sparked the most interest, the most controversy, and the most currently popular efforts to understand her poetry in the specific context of LGBTQIA assumptions.

Dickinson herself might well be both disappointed and strongly opposed to any of the myriad attempts to decode the meaning of her poems by such conjectural methods. She was a woman who jealously guarded her privacy. And it is also important to remember that she was a genius in her own right. While neither confirming nor denying any of the theories about her that the many disparate readings of her work have suggested, one must always be mindful of the fact that her reality may have been both more complex and more profound than any of the scenarios forwarded by scholars.

We do know that cultivating a close and emotional bond with Dickinson was not typical, nor was it easy. To illustrate this, Steve spoke of Thomas Wentworth Higginson, the publisher who encouraged Dickinson's efforts as a poet and who would later become personally involved in printing her work posthumously. He met her only twice, yet after visiting her, he was reported to have observed to a friend, "I never was with anyone who drained my mind power so much." In a similar vein, one of the girls who had known her since childhood wrote about Emily at the time of her death, "She loved with all her might...." These two observations have become of central importance to me in examining the assertion being considered here.

Of course, Dickinson did indeed experience tragic disappointments in her personal life, disappointments that may have led to the ultimate reclusiveness of her later years. As usual, her poetry is eloquent:

My life closed twice before its close;
It yet remains to see
If immortality unveil
A third event to me,

So huge, so hopeless to conceive
As these that twice befell.

Parting is all we know of heaven,
And all we need of hell.

A question worth asking here, however, may be, to what sort of 'parting' does this poem refer? For years the answer forwarded by critics and scholars has been to a devastating separation from a romantic partner. This may be the case, but it is not the only possible answer.

Surely one of the greatest challenges faced by any person of genius is an inevitable state of loneliness. That this loneliness *is* unavoidable is the result of the fact that no one can see and experience the world in precisely the way that a man or woman of genius sees and experiences it. Yet this fact did not prevent Emily from yearning for the companionship of other people who could appreciate and value her talents and abilities.

Many Dickinson biographers have attempted to identify the people about whom they believe the poet must have been thinking when she penned "My life closed twice." The first two candidates most often agreed upon are Benjamin Franklin Newton and Charles Wadsworth. Yet the fact that Emily also appeared to foresee the possibility of a "third event" to place along with these first two has encouraged current scholars to suggest yet another person to consider: her longtime friend and sister-in-law, Susan Huntington Gilbert Dickinson.

Each of these people's relationships to Emily was unique, and with each, Emily found herself passionately involved, but the nature and extent of her feelings elude simple explanation.

To Benjamin Franklin Newton, the "friend who taught me immortality," Emily owed her introduction to books and writers that comprised the world's greatest literary achievements. Newton showed his respect for her talent and intellect by sharing with her masterpieces of literature she had not previously encountered. His faith in her strengthened her belief in herself and deeply endeared him to her. Some scholars saw in the intense nature of her correspondence with him clear evidence of a growing infatuation.

Charles Wadsworth, her "dearest earthly friend," was a Presbyterian minister in Philadelphia whom Dickinson personally met only twice. Himself a shy and retiring man, in the pulpit his passionate sermons left his congregation with a feeling that their minister had experienced "years of conflict and agony," but that his faith was all the more remarkable as a result of being so sorely tried. Emily described him as "a dusk gem, born of troubled waters." Yet exactly what in him so moved Dickinson has remained something of a mystery.

Susan Huntington Gilbert, Dickinson's "Only Woman in the World," was Emily's dearest personal friend whose initial relationship was described as a "tempest of intimacy." They took long walks together, shared poetry, and at first were virtually inseparable. Many modern critics see here clear evidence of Dickinson's lesbian yearnings, also reflected in their correspondence.

Yet from each of these three sensitive and kindred souls, Dickinson would find herself "closed" off. Newton would move away from Amherst to begin his law practice and marry, though he died before reaching the age of 35. Wadsworth, already a married man with children, would resign from his Philadelphia church to take another posting in San Francisco. Susan Gilbert would leave Amherst for a year and a half to teach school in Baltimore, and when she returned, would marry Emily's brother and move into the house next door where she and Austin would raise three children.

It is impossible to know for certain why these "parting" experiences occurred. Newton's death, of course, was untimely and tragic. But why did Wadsworth transplant himself thousands of miles away from his East Coast congregation? Had he sensed an uncomfortable intensity building up in his epistolary friendship with Emily, an intensity from which he felt a need to distance himself? Did Susan become aware of a level of intimacy in the letters Emily sent her to which she was not inclined to respond? Was it too overwhelming to be "loved with all [Emily's] might"? Or, as Thomas Higginson had observed, simply too exhausting to be in close proximity to a woman "who drained my mind power so much"? It appears that intimate friendships with sensitive and appreciative souls were destined to be denied to this extraordinary woman, Emily Dickinson.

Assertion #5) She was regarded as a "strange woman" by the citizens of Amherst, and no one was aware of her habit of writing poetry until her scribbled verses were published after her death.

This is another assertion which is simultaneously accurate and misleading. Particularly in her later, more reclusive, years, there undoubtedly were people living in Amherst who wondered about this secretive woman clothed in white. But, Steve informed us, this hadn't always been the case. In fact, the Dickinson home had been known in town as a wonderful source of fresh vegetables and flowers grown in the garden that Emily tended. Furthermore, she had a reputation of being a superb baker, and her pastries were quite popular in town. So the accuracy of this assertion depends largely on the time of Emily's life that is being referred to and the individual personality of the "citizen" in question.

Perhaps the most misleading part of this assertion regards the assumption that the people of Amherst were unaware of Dickinson's habit of writing poetry. It is true that Emily kept in her room a private cache of poems gathered together in sewn packets. However, Steve informed us, Emily's poetry was widely known by anyone who purchased her flowers, vegetables, and pastries. She frequently wrapped these items in scraps of paper onto which she had written verses.

Yet the assertion is accurate in that, while her customers were aware that Emily had written short poems on the paper in which she wrapped her wares, almost no one in town took them seriously as personal observations and revelations that would change the face of American literature. Her verses were usually short, and they were frequently witty. One thinks of such perfect poems as this one:

I'm nobody! Who are you?
Are you nobody, too?
Then there's a pair of us--don't tell!
They'd banish us, you know.

How dreary to be somebody!
How public like a frog
To tell your name the livelong day
To an admiring bog!

What her customers from Amherst failed to acknowledge, then, was not the existence of Dickinson's poetry, but rather the fact that some of what she was writing—and casually handing to them on pieces of wrapping paper—was poetry inspired by genius. It would take years for her poems to be collected, printed in book form, and praised by scholars who would teach readers to appreciate their subtlety and beauty. Steve mentioned that, even today, someone in Amherst occasionally comes across a piece of paper containing verses written in Emily's hand, a paper that had been saved and stowed away for safe keeping.

Dickinson's final years were reclusive, withdrawn from society. She still would sit at her desk by the window looking northward toward Austin and Susan's home, the Evergreens, but she had long since ceased to venture across the lawn, even when they gave parties for such touring celebrities as Ralph Waldo Emerson and Harriet Beecher Stowe.

Visitors to the Dickinson home today have the opportunity to pay to reserve an hour of time when they can sit by themselves in her room and reflect and write on the same desk in the same spot where she had created some of her greatest works.

Yet ultimately, regardless of her personal confinement and her ruminations about death and dying, regardless of her spiritual doubts and the pain of her losses and difficult partings, regardless even of publishers' unwillingness to print her verses, Emily Dickinson knew her poetry had great value. It was forever hers. It never died nor deserted her. Her poetry had become her world. And as Steve had so perceptively discerned, more than anything else, it was "the world she wanted."

8

Harriet Beecher Stowe

Crucible, Elixir, Clarion

Stowe's Home in Hartford, CT

Stowe House in Cincinnati, OH

Crucible

So far, everything had gone according to plan. Carol and I had taken the morning to drive from St. Louis to Cincinnati, Ohio, to visit the Harriet Beecher Stowe house. We arrived just after lunch and purchased tickets for the next tour of the home. While we waited, I visited the site gift shop and asked a knowledgeable worker there--who I'll name Diane--what I thought was a simple question. "Which room in the house was Mrs. Stowe's?" Her answer perplexed me. "Actually, Harriet never lived here for very long, and she certainly didn't have a room exclusively to herself."

"So, *was* this Harriet Beecher Stowe's house?" I asked.

"Well," Diane began. "Yes and no. I understand that may sound confusing, but the truth is that this home *was* very important to Harriet Beecher Stowe. It *was* an essential part of the years of her life that she spent in Cincinnati. However, it was not a home owned by her family."

Diane could sense my perplexity. She quickly added, "Let me explain this from the beginning. Do you have a couple of minutes?"

I answered that I was waiting for the next tour and that, as a writer working on a book about authors' homes, I would appreciate anything she had to say. She smiled as she saw me open my notebook and fish a pen out of my pocket.

"We'll have just enough time, then. The first thing you need to know is that this home was never a personal residence. It was built as the parsonage for the newly formed Lane Theological Seminary here in Cincinnati. Lyman Beecher, Harriet's father, had answered the call to become its first president. So this lovely dwelling never technically belonged to him but was the housing provided for the Seminary's head officer. There were, of course, rooms available for his family, and Harriet, along with several other of her siblings, accompanied Lyman as he began his work. But Harriet was a young woman, twenty-two years old, when this home was finally finished in 1833. Her goal was to become a teacher and, after she lived here a short while, she moved to an apartment closer to her work in town.

"Of course, she was a frequent visitor here, and she became well aware of the debates and disputes regarding slavery and abolition that raged among the students in the Seminary.

"Then three years later, in 1836," Diane pointed down the center hall of the building, "Harriet married Calvin Stowe in the front parlor of this house. As it turned out, she then spent several months living here during the first year of her marriage. You see, Mr. Stowe had already committed himself to a trip to Europe to study public education there, and, of course, he had planned to take Harriet with him. However, she became pregnant and decided not to risk the perils of a long sea voyage. She returned here to the parsonage for the duration of her pregnancy. In November of 1836, she gave birth to twin girls in a small room upstairs. When Calvin returned from Europe, he and Harriet moved into their own lodgings where the young family could begin their settled life together. So you see now why I had to answer your question, 'yes and no.' "

Diane smiled and added an important final thought. "The Stowes stayed here in town for another 13 years, until 1850, when Mr. Stowe was invited to teach at his alma mater, Bowdoin College in Brunswick, Maine. But what an important period in Harriet's life this had been. Without her years living here in Cincinnati, she never would have—never really *could have*—written *Uncle Tom's Cabin*." I thanked this articulate and fascinating raconteur for her time and information, and I walked toward the front parlor where I knew Carol was waiting for me.

But I kept thinking about Diane's last statement. I felt instinctively that she was right. In Connecticut where Harriet had been born and had grown up, slavery was seen as a societal problem existent only in the distant Southern states, a topic to be discussed at meetings throughout New England where virtually everyone in attendance agreed with each other. In Cincinnati matters were different. On the nearby hillsides and plantations of Kentucky, slavery was an immediate and visible reality. Slave catchers looking for runaways were a common sight. Yet simultaneously a variety of routes on the underground railroad had also sprung up, offering aid to escaping blacks as they fled further north to freedom. For the citizens of Southern Ohio, then, both slavery and abolitionism were facts of life, and even more importantly, were sometimes causes of death for those involved personally with them.

I was born and raised in Cincinnati, and as a result I knew firsthand how the region had played a significant role in 19th century American history. Here in Cincinnati the Ohio River narrows as it wends its way westward toward the Mississippi, flowing between steep hills on either side of its channel. This makes the river's current swift here, but it also brings the two shores agonizingly close for anyone on one side desiring to escape to the other. The proximity of the slave state of Kentucky and the free state of Ohio created a natural point of conflict over this contentious issue that was threatening to tear apart the entire nation.

On the north bank of the Ohio, just east of Cincinnati in the small village of Point Pleasant, a young man named Jesse Grant was taught the tannery trade by his neighbor, Owen Brown. Brown's son John would become the nation's most widely known abolitionist. In later years Jesse's son Ulysses would also play a vital role in settling the national debate over slavery. He would serve his country as Commanding General of the Union Army in the Civil War.

My maternal grandmother remembered one particular winter in her youth when the temperatures were so bitterly cold that the entire surface of the Ohio River had frozen over, and horse drawn sleighs had been able to pass to the other side without difficulty. Almost every year saw winter days where ice fragments could be seen floating downstream, a phenomenon that Harriet Beecher Stowe would make particularly memorable in *Uncle Tom's Cabin* when the slave mother, Eliza, escapes from her pursuers by making her way across the river atop shifting pieces of ice.

Southern Ohio, then, was the crucible into which Harriet Beecher Stowe found herself planted for eighteen critical years of her young womanhood. It would provide her with the greatest topic of her life and the substance of her most important literary achievement. As she herself would write in the concluding chapter of her famous novel, "The separate incidents that compose the narrative are, to a very great extent, authentic, occurring, many of them, either under her own observation, or that of her personal friends" (625). Without her years spent in Cincinnati, none of such "authentic" accounts of slavery and the slave trade could have been stored in the reservoir of her life's experiences. *Uncle Tom's Cabin* might never have been written.

Stowe Home in Brunswick, ME

Elixir

In 1850, Harriet Beecher Stowe moved into this comfortable rental home on Federal Street in Brunswick, Maine, near the campus of Bowdoin College where her husband had been appointed to be a professor of religion. In addition to the family's personal belongings, she brought with her two indelible memories from her life in Ohio.

The first of these two memories came from the early years of her residence in Cincinnati. Soon after her arrival there, she had begun to work as a teacher. In 1833, one of her pupils, a girl named Elizabeth Marshall Key, invited her to visit her family home in nearby Washington, Kentucky. During this visit, Elizabeth's father took Harriet to the courthouse lawn in Maysville, where she witnessed for the first time a slave auction. The experience was brutally affecting to the young teacher. In Cincinnati, even at the theological seminary her father was heading, slavery was a hot political topic. But here in Maysville, it was an established physical reality. Stowe would later write about this visit into slave country as being forever seared into her memory. It would also become her earliest inspiration for *Uncle Tom's Cabin*.

The second memory Stowe had brought with her from Ohio was a recent and tragically personal loss: the death of her youngest child, Charles Samuel, who had died during an epidemic of cholera that swept through Cincinnati in 1849. Harriet was disconsolate as a result of his passing. She felt that she could never fully survive this loss unless somehow it could lead her into imparting a significant blessing to others. But what could she do to bring about such a blessing? This question, along with her grief, accompanied her to her new home in Maine where two additional incidents would lead her inescapably to the answer she was seeking.

The first occurred in the very year of her arrival in Brunswick. The Fugitive Slave Law had been passed into national law in 1850. Now southern slave owners could legally travel north to apprehend their stolen "property," individual slaves who had managed to escape to the free states. And to one such escaped slave, John Andrew Jackson, the passage of this inhumane law had sounded a personal alarm. He realized that he was now liable to legal apprehension and a forcible return to slavery in South Carolina. The prospect was unthinkable to him, and he decided to head north to Canada where, if he could make his way across the border, he would be truly free.

He traveled north from Massachusetts, passing into the state of Maine and found his way to Brunswick, where, he would later write:

> *During my flight from Salem to Canada, I met with a very sincere friend and helper, who gave me a refuge dur-*

ing the night, and set me on my way. Her name was Mrs. Beecher Stowe.

Jackson added the following details in his autobiography, published in 1862:

She took me in and fed me, and gave me some clothes and five dollars. She also inspected my back, which is covered with scars which I shall carry with me to the grave. She listened with great interest to my story, and sympathized with me when I told her how long I had been parted from my wife Louisa and my daughter Jennie, and perhaps, forever.

Once again, just as she had witnessed it at the slave market in Kentucky years earlier, Stowe was encountering personally the terrible results of slavery. Only now she herself was a grieving mother, feeling the agony of her own forced separation from her precious son, Charley. She gave Jackson the help he needed to continue his ultimately successful journey to Canada, but this brief encounter only deepened the importance of her soul-searching question: What could she do to transform the tragedies she had both witnessed and lived through personally into a larger blessing for mankind?

In February of 1851 she received her answer in a strikingly dramatic way.

While attending a Sunday Communion service at the nearby First Parish Church, Harriet experienced what she identified as a "vision." Instead of the image of the crucified Christ Jesus, however, Stowe saw four figures: an older male slave being whipped to death by two other slaves, directed in their cruel task by a vicious white man. This experience was so powerful that, upon returning to the house on Federal Street, Stowe immediately began to set down an account of the vision. She would describe doing so "as if what she wrote was blown through her mind as with the rushing of a mighty wind." Her question had been answered. What she could do was write. The book that would result from her Communion vision, the book she later observed that God had "imposed on her," would prove to be the elixir needed to cure the disease of slavery. *Uncle Tom's Cabin* had been conceived.

During her years in Ohio, Stowe had written several stories that had been published, stories that taught moral lessons. But now she was writing with a fervor she had never before experienced. Some of her family's memories of that first day give the account that she wrote continuously until she had run out of paper, and then she continued to write on the brown paper in which groceries had been recently delivered to the house. This work was a mission, not simply an exercise in imagination.

Soon she wrote a letter to Gamaliel Bailey, the editor of the *National Era*, an abolitionist newspaper, in which she urged him to publish a series of sketches, perhaps three or four, which would illustrate the horrors of slavery. Her letter demonstrates the level of her dedication to the task:

> *Up to this year I have always felt that I had no particular call to meddle with this subject, and I dreaded to expose even my own mind to the full force of its exciting power. But I feel now that the time is come when even a woman or a child who can speak a word for freedom and humanity is bound to speak...and I hope every woman who can write will not be silent.*

Bailey was clearly impressed, and in the June 5, 1851, issue of the *National Era*, the first installment of *Uncle Tom's Cabin* appeared.

But it wasn't long before it became apparent that Stowe's work would extend far beyond the three or four installments she had originally planned. Ultimately *Uncle Tom's Cabin* would be comprised of forty installments and would take until April of 1852 to reach its final episode.

The house where she wrote it still stands on Federal Street and is now the property of Bowdoin College which uses its upper level for faculty offices. Its two front parlors are open for tourist visits. As one faces the house from Federal Street, its left, or northern, front parlor was the place where Harriet taught school for professors' children. The south parlor across the entry hall is the room most identified with her novel.

When Carol and I toured these rooms in August of 2017, it was referred to as "Harriet's Reading Room," though today it is called "Harriet's Writing Room." It will probably never be known whether or not she actually wrote in this room or somewhere upstairs, but most certainly this southern parlor was the place where, on regular occasions, Stowe would invite Bowdoin students or others interested in following the ongoing process of her writing of *Uncle Tom's Cabin* as it was appearing in the *National Era*, to come to listen and comment upon the latest installment before its publication.

No list was ever made to record the names of the people who attended these readings, but we know of one young Bowdoin student who was sometimes there and who himself would come to play a significant part in the history of his nation: Joshua Lawrence Chamberlain. Some eleven years in the future, in 1863, on a swelteringly hot hillside just outside the town of Gettysburg, he would order a maneuver that would turn the tide of battle irrevocably in favor of the Union Army, and four years later he would be elected the thirty-second Governor of the State of Maine.

The novel that he and the other attendees were following with great interest centered around two distinct stories. The first was the tale of a slave woman, Eliza, her husband, George, and her child, Harry, all of whom were trying to escape the slave state of Kentucky and make their way to Canada and freedom. The second followed the life of Tom, a beloved—and valuable—slave who was sold down river and first became a beloved servant in a New Orleans household only later to be made an abused and tormented field hand on a cotton plantation in Arkansas.

Uncle Tom's Cabin is a work of great complexity, and this may explain why it has become both the most well-known historical novel ever written in America and the least read work in that canon. The picture it paints refuses to succumb to the stereotypes we have come to expect in narratives having to do with slavery. All its white characters are not monsters, though some, most notably, Simon Legree, Tom's last master, certainly deserve that title. But Augustine St. Clare, another white character in the book, is a caring, gentle soul who treats Tom with respect and sympathy. Some of the black characters are perfectly willing to collude with their white masters in punishing other slaves.

Yet Eliza, George, and Harry do stand for the best of humanity in a world cursed with slavery. Even one of the white characters who abhors "the peculiar institution," Miss Ophelia, finds herself expressing racist views as she becomes frustrated with her new charge, a black girl named Topsy. In short, Stowe never flinches from depicting the contradictions and inconsistencies of both sides in her tract depicting the horrors of slavery.

Standing here in the parlor where Harriet Beecher Stowe had read aloud her novel, the book which, according to legend, Abraham Lincoln himself had identified as the chief catalyst of the "great war" toward which the nation was hurtling, both Carol and I felt the profound significance of this place. Here, in this sun-washed room, a work of literature had instigated one of the most critical moments of American history. Here, one woman acting under the force of what she understood to be a divine impulse, had dared to create a story that would inspire its readers to demand an end to human slavery.

Uncle Tom's Cabin was so widely read that it was published in book form a month before its final installment appeared in the *National Era*. Although her limited financial means had forced her to accept a mere 10% of the profits it generated, the novel made Stowe a wealthy woman. Stowe cleared $10,300 in the first three months of its publication. 300,000 copies were sold in the United States in its first year; its British sales more than quadrupled that number.

Not all of the book's many readers agreed with its sentiments, however. While the vast majority of its audience found themselves profoundly moved by the hardships of its characters struggling to be free, Southern readers argued that her depiction of slavery was a terrible distortion. There were even some Northern writers and free blacks who questioned her presumption in assuming herself capable of creating black characters as if she were qualified to speak for them.

In response to some of the criticisms she was receiving, Stowe wrote an important letter explaining her intentions:

> *I wrote what I did because as a woman, as a mother, I was oppressed and broken-hearted with the sorrows and injustice I saw, because as a Christian I felt the dishonor to Christianity—because as a lover of my country, I trembled at the coming day of wrath.*

In 1853, Calvin Stowe was offered a teaching position at the prestigious Andover Theological Seminary in Newton, Massachusetts. He left Bowdoin and Brunswick, taking Harriet and the family with him. Once again the Stowes were on the move.

Stowe Home in Hartford, CT

Clarion

Harriet, now a nationally prominent literary figure, would live for another forty-four years subsequent to the publication of *Uncle Tom's Cabin*. Before settling at Andover, she and Calvin traveled to Europe where she was greeted as a celebrity. This was particularly the case in England where she made the acquaintance of several literary figures, including the novelist George Eliot. After the family's return to the United States and Calvin's assumption of his professorial duties, she would have the opportunity to meet Abraham Lincoln in 1862, at the very darkest hour of the American Civil War. She would write several other books, but none of them would approach the importance of *Uncle Tom's Cabin*.

Calvin retired from teaching at Andover in 1864, and soon thereafter the Stowes relocated to Connecticut, the state where Harriet had been born. Using the money she had earned over the preceding decade, Stowe oversaw the construction of her dream home in the Nook Farm area of Hartford, a home she named "Oakholm." This house no longer stands. The family would live there until 1870.

In 1867, in an effort to help their son Frederick William recover both from wounds he had incurred during his service in the Union Army and from his addiction to alcohol, the Stowes purchased a citrus farm for him on the St. Johns River in northeastern Florida. They hoped this change of setting, together with the responsibilities involved with running the operations of the farm, would regenerate and redirect the arc of his life. Unfortunately, Fred was a poor businessman, and the enterprise failed after only a year of his management. His drinking continued until his early death.

But Florida came to have a great charm for the famous novelist. Just across the St. Johns River from the citrus farm she and Calvin had purchased for Fred, she discovered the town of Mandarin and a lovely property consisting of a cottage located on thirty acres of orange groves. The Stowes bought it and, for several years, wintered there. That home no longer stands, but Harriet's book *Palmetto Leaves* is a wonderfully descriptive narrative that recounts the beauty she found and the activities she enjoyed in this semitropical locale.

By 1870, however, the expenses of maintaining Oakholm led the Stowes to one last move. Their new address was located just a few blocks north, but it was a considerably more modest setting. Both Harriet and Calvin would live here for the rest of their lives, he until 1886 and she for ten years longer. It is this home at 77 Forest Street that tourists frequent today.

Carol and I have visited this location twice, most recently in the summer of 2017. It is a fascinating composite of a careful restoration of a late 19th century Victorian era home and an obvious effort by the Harriet Beecher Stowe Center, also located on this property, to update and make relevant to modern audiences the life and work of a writer whose reputation has been questioned over the years.

Regarding the restoration, the care taken to decorate several rooms in the house in exactly the way they looked when the Stowes lived here is most impressive. In one parlor, both the furniture and some of the works of art hanging on the walls have been placed exactly where they appear in a displayed period photograph of Stowe sitting in the very room where visitors are standing.

Upstairs, Stowe's bedroom/study is particularly poignant, with its single bed and her writing table pulled close to the bay windows at the rear of the house. For such a heralded writer, one might assume that this painstaking recreation of her world would be all that would be necessary to acknowledge and celebrate her remarkable achievements. Yet it didn't work out quite that way. Why not?

Because Harriet Beecher Stowe's novel has remained uncomfortably controversial. Already noted, of course, were the original Southern critics who leveled objections to the book for its harsh depictions of slavery and the Northern blacks who felt Stowe unqualified to portray black characters. But even after the war had been fought and won and the 13th, 14th, and 15th amendments had been added to the Bill of Rights, *Uncle Tom's Cabin* attracted pointed attacks from the very people it had been written to help.

In the 20th century, some influential black authors had continued to attack the book. Most notably in 1949 James Baldwin argued that Stowe's novel both presented negative stereotypes of blacks and then urged them to be acquiescent under the tyranny of their white overlords. Tom, for instance, rather than rising up in a manful way to oppose the injustices inflicted upon him, refuses to fight his oppressors. This response might appease whites, Baldwin argued, but it set the worst possible example for American blacks.

Then a decade or so later, would come Malcolm X, the Black Panthers, widespread Civil Rights protests, and the urban riots of the 60's, as well as ongoing outbursts of violence in response to continuing instances of racism and prejudice. In such a climate, what were the keepers of Harriet Beecher Stowe's memory to do?

What the Center here in Hartford has attempted to do has been to acknowledge and give voice to the various divergent opinions surrounding Stowe's novel and to position the site as a kind of sounding board for the correction of the sorts of injustices she had fought against throughout her life. In doing so, the Center is attempting to keep Stowe's work relevant to its 21st century audience. And this tactic appears to be succeeding. In the kitchen area of the home, tour groups are given paper and markers and are invited to identify today's social needs. The resultant display of visitors' comments include a large number of pieces of paper posing such concerns as "equal rights," "equal pay," "gender neutrality," and "Black Lives Matter."

Yet it is also undeniable that this new direction moves the focus of the home away from Harriet Beecher Stowe herself. And, in some ways, that would appear most justifiable. After all, the groundwork of her greatest contribution to history had been laid in Cincinnati, Ohio, and the composition of the novel that had made her famous took place in Brunswick, Maine. Here in Hartford, although she lived in this home for the last twenty-three years of her life, she came to be in a pronounced state of decline. However, there was one activity of her final years in this home in Hartford that challenges thought. Historian Jim Bernhard explains how "Harriet Beecher Stowe spent the last years of her life in a demented state writing her great novel *Uncle Tom's Cabin* over and over. She wrote subconsciously from memory, word for word, as if she were creating it for the first time."

This certainly suggests an aberrant state of mind, but it also implicitly poses a simple question: why would she do such a thing as repeatedly write her novel from memory "over and over…word for word"? While that question is unanswerable, it led me to reconsider her response to the first group of critics she had faced: "I wrote what I did because as a woman, as a mother, I was oppressed and broken-hearted with the sorrows and injustice I saw, *because as a Christian I felt the dishonor to Christianity*—because as a lover of my country, I trembled at the coming day of wrath." [my emphasis]

It may be significant that the overwhelming majority of opinions regarding both Stowe and *Uncle Tom's Cabin* tend to discount or at best marginalize the italicized section of the above quotation. Harriet Beecher Stowe is widely lauded as a groundbreaking woman writer. The significance of the tragedy of the death of her young son Charley has been widely discussed and well documented. Her recoil from the injustice of slavery has never been questioned, nor has her sincere love of her country. But what people, especially those in the 20th and 21st centuries, tend not to discuss is her dedication to Christianity.

Yet Christianity, it is easy to argue, was in fact the dominant influence in her life.

Her family, of course, was a collection of ministers, preachers and teachers. But it is the very text of *Uncle Tom's Cabin* itself that identifies the need for spiritual, as well as societal, salvation. Both the characters of Eva, the angelic child of the St. Claire family, and Tom are dedicated to the spiritual reclamation of the people around them. The dying Eva addresses the servants in her household with the ardor of a saint:

> I want to speak to you about your souls...Many of you, I am afraid, are very careless. You are thinking only about this world. I want you to remember that there is a beautiful world, where Jesus is. I am going there, and you can go there. It is for you, as much as me. But, if you want to go there, you must not live idle, careless, thoughtless lives. You must be Christians. (410)

Her subsequent gift to each of them is a lock of her hair. But, she adds, rather than being simply a personal reminder of herself, she hopes these mementos will help them to recall her words and to live their lives more spiritually.

And Tom, after suffering untold anguish at the hands of two of Simon Legree's black henchmen, tells his old master's son who has come from Kentucky to save him, "O, Mas'r George, ye're too late. The Lord's bought me, and is going to take me home,--and I long to go. Heaven is better than Kentuck...I've got the victory!–the Lord Jesus has given it to me! Glory be to His name!" (594) With his dying breath, Tom forgives and spiritually directs his now repentant torturers toward the Christianity of which they had been ignorant before.

Finally Stowe herself steps out from her narrative and makes the case without the guise of fiction:

> Pity him not! Such a life and death is not for pity! Not in the riches of omnipotence is the chief glory of God; but in self-denying, suffering love! And blessed are the men whom he calls to fellowship with him, bearing their cross after him with patience. Of such it is written, "Blessed

are they that mourn, for they shall be comforted." (598)

For Stowe, then, Christian salvation was of even greater importance than the emancipation of the slaves. Here she addresses her audience neither as free men nor as slaves, but simply as human beings, all of whom have the opportunity to be called to fellowship with Christ.

Did she sense, in her final years, that this larger message had been misunderstood, even neglected? That somehow the true goal of her abolitionist novel had been missed by readers too easily satisfied with "thinking only about this world"?

We will never know, but her dedication to writing her book from memory, over and over, word for word, suggests that, at the very least, she understood the vital importance of its spiritual message. This was the blessing for which, as a grieving mother, she had so earnestly prayed. And this was the clarion call she wanted to declare until the end of her days. She did so, in spite of the state of her conscious mind. Her determination was a testament to her devotion, as an author, as a mother, and as a woman, to the betterment --and salvation--of mankind.

9

Mark Twain

"The first group is less crowded."

Mark Twain's Home in Hartford, CT

In the Summer of 2000, I, my wife Carol, and our two children, Katie and Andy, arrived at the St. Louis airport to board an international flight to England. For me this was a business trip, as I had been assigned to give a speech in Surrey. It was also, however, a family vacation, our first trip to Europe since the children had been born.

We landed at Gatwick Airport near London, and, upon exiting the plane, I headed to a currency exchange location to turn my American dollars into English pounds. Imagine my surprise when I looked at the ten pound notes I received and found the image of the Queen on one side of the bill (which was to be expected), but Charles Dickens pictured on the reverse side. An author on currency? "What a great country," I found myself saying aloud, as I showed the note to Carol and the kids.

Then came to my mind the inevitable question: If the United States had decided to do something similar, which of our writers should have received this honor? To me the answer was obvious: Mark Twain.

I was an English teacher for thirty-seven years, more than thirty of which were spent living in Missouri, and after my retirement in 2010, my wife and I have continued to make our home there. The writings of Mark Twain have been a central interest in both my intellectual and professional life. He is Missouri's literary crown jewel, and the state boasts both the geography and several individual locales that he made famous through his writings. Ron Powers, a recent biographer, labeled him the great "American voice."

But in these days of racial upheavals and protest marches, Twain would appear to be much too controversial a choice. And ironically enough, that's been the case long before our present moment in time.

Twain's widely acknowledged masterpiece, *The Adventures of Huckleberry Finn*, has been periodically banned since its very first appearance in print. The initial criticism of the book was aimed chiefly at its title character. Huck Finn, critics argued, was an inveterate liar, a rough-hewn delinquent whose language was so raw and ungrammatical that it was completely inappropriate for the ears and eyes of younger readers. It would take nearly a hundred years for scholars and linguists to arrive at a consensus regarding the value and accuracy of Twain's incorporation of language as spoken by rural Americans into the lexicon of our literature.

In the meantime, however, another much more serious charge was beginning to be aimed at *The Adventures of Huckleberry Finn*. The book was accused of being a racist text. The proof? Twain's use of the "n" word throughout the novel. In fact, this objectionable and pejorative term appears more often in *The Adventures of Huckleberry Finn* than in the combined total of all Twain's other works.

The question is—or at least should be—why? And the answer to that question is important because, despite the use of this charged and hurtful word, *The Adventures of Huckleberry Finn* is actually Twain's most powerful attack *against* racism and racist attitudes.

The entire arc of Twain's narrative shows Huck's gradual ascent out of the racist notions with which he was surrounded as a child. With each passing incident in his life on the run with Jim, an escaping slave, Huck becomes increasingly aware of Jim's humanity and dignity. So much so that in the novel's moral climax, Huck finally concludes that he would rather literally "go to hell" than surrender his friend, Jim, to the slavecatchers.

Mark Twain himself, as both speaker and benefactor, was an outspoken proponent of black individuals. He appeared on stage with Booker T. Washington at a time when doing so elicited death threats from enraged segregationists. Twain also anonymously helped pay for the Yale Law School education of Warner T. McGuinn, a black man who would later mentor a young Thurgood Marshall, who himself would become the first black member of the Supreme Court of the United States.

Samuel Clemens was no racist. But he was a complex and sometimes contradictory man. His chosen pen name, Mark Twain, was much more than a simple reference to the call of a steamboat's leadsman, "mark twain" or "two fathoms," meaning eight feet of depth over which the boat could pass easily. In fact, that leadsman's call itself had two very different, even contradictory, meanings. If, prior to the call of "mark twain," the measure of the river bed had been "no bottom," then the meaning of "mark twain" was that the water was starting to shallow, hence becoming more potentially dangerous. If, on the other hand, the call had followed a warning of dangerously low water, "mark twain" would be a comforting assurance of deepening depth and, hence, safer passage. This dichotomy of meanings suggests that this pen name was a perfect reflection of the complexity of the man. Twain's first biographer, Albert Bigelow Paine, would often refer to his subject's "many-sided character" (1271). Twain's daughter Clara was a bit more abrupt, calling her father's frequent changes of mood indications of his "healthfully inconsistent disposition" (Clemens 16). How, then, can anyone hope to arrive at a substantive understanding of this complicated man?

If he is to be found anywhere, it must be in his writings. But to comprehend the writings, it is also helpful to know the places which had inspired them. These locations sometimes reveal his deepest insights, desires, and fears, as well as his understanding of the world and his place within it.

There are six such "Inspiration Points" that are particularly worth visiting. Four of them are located in the state of Missouri, another is in Hartford, Connecticut, and the sixth can be found in the hills north of Elmira, New York, near the southern border of that state and Pennsylvania. Getting to know these places has prepared me for a closer analysis of his books, two of which, *Life on the Mississippi* and *Following the Equator*, I have come to regard as essential aids in appreciating the mind of this remarkable man. Both are autobiographical, the first written in the years of his greatest literary creativity and the second constituting his last fully realized subscription-sized volume of his later years. Both will be addressed in the pages to come.

[This chapter differs from the others in three key ways. First, it culminates a thirty-year-long interest in the life and works of Mark Twain. Second, it includes visits to six separate locales, each having a significant impact on Twain's life and thought. (Hence, the six separate sections into which this chapter is divided.) And third, this chapter includes materials which I wrote for inclusion in three volumes of essays that were privately published as part of The Mark Twain Project at Principia School (2005-2010).]

Florida, Missouri (1835-1839): "...almost invisible..."

In his autobiographical writings, Twain noted that "I was born on the 30th of November, 1835, in the almost invisible village of Florida, Monroe County, Missouri" (1). And nothing much has changed there since then. When I first visited the site of his birth, there was but one resident identified in the latest census of the town, and she died within the next year. Today its population is still listed as zero, though a few vacation homes have been built within the town limits, close to the shores of the man-made Mark Twain Lake, the result of damming the nearby Salt River that had run past the village at the time of Twain's birth.

The location of the small two room cabin in which Sam Clemens had been born is memorialized by a squared granite marker in a field next to what was once the main street in town. It is one of only two pieces of evidence in Florida that the Clemens family had ever lived here.

The second is located in the nearby cemetery where a simple headstone identifies the resting place of Twain's older sister, Margaret, who died before Sam had reached the age of four.

Nothing much remains of the town and the buildings that once fronted the main street. There is, however, an important treasure to be found nearby, a treasure that contains not a replica but the actual two room home in which Samuel Clemens had been born in 1835.

Birthplace cabin of Samuel Clemens in Florida, MO

Although obviously not an important setting for Twain as a writer, as he was a young child when his family moved to Hannibal in 1839, this house must have provided him with a memory of, and even a testament to, the social level from which he had sprung. For the rest of his life, Clemens would work tirelessly to provide both for himself and for his family a lifestyle and level of luxury and affluence that would ensure that the poverty and deprivation of his humble beginnings would never be repeated.

It is impossible to know with any degree of certainty whether the small cradle on display in the bedroom of this modest cabin had ever really held the baby Samuel Clemens. But the splendor and grandeur of the home he would construct for Livy Langdon in Hartford, Connecticut, more than attested to his desire to be a part of a level of society which had not been available to the Clemens family of Florida, Missouri. If it did nothing else for him, any memory he had of this humble site would be a constant reminder of a life of which he no longer wanted to be a part.

Yet even this simple cabin has come to have another important meaning. Its preservation was the result of the tireless labors of Merritt Violette, the grandson of a woman who, in her teens, had been present at the birth of Sam Clemens. Yet the fact of its continued existence exemplifies a respect for, and admiration of, the memory of the great writer that baby would become.

This cabin, then, like Clemens himself, is "twain." It symbolizes the poverty and difficult circumstances of his early life, a life he was determined to leave behind. But it is also a symbol of the love and esteem of those who came to know and value his contribution to the literature of his country and the world.

Quarles Farm (1843-1848): "...a heavenly place for a boy."

View from Quarles Farm near Florida, MO

About four miles northwest of Florida, Sam Clemens's uncle, John Quarles, owned a farm of approximately 500 acres. Here, in the summers of 1843 to 1848 the Clemens children were invited to stay and enjoy the activities and freedom of the land. There were rolling hills, nearby forests and streams, an infinite number of opportunities for youthful adventures. In his autobiographical remembrances, Twain would identify this site as having been "...a heavenly place for a boy" (5).

Replica of Quarles Farmhouse

The current owner of the land, Karen Hunt, has made it her goal to memorialize this setting so important to the young Samuel Clemens. For several years she hosted students from nearby colleges to come to the site of the farmhouse and conduct archeological digs to uncover artifacts related to the period of time when the Quarles family lived and worked here. Then more recently, she has overseen the construction of a replica of the farmhouse on its original location.

Her interest, however, is not confined solely to the importance of this home to the life of Samuel Clemens. She is also very interested in reproducing the unique architectural elements of this early dwelling. To this end Twain's vivid remembrance of the house has been a great aid in her efforts to reconstruct it accurately.

On the day of my visit to the site, I was invited to make my way up to the second floor where Sam Clemens would have stayed while he summered here. The exposed walls still revealed angled wooden blocks that allowed the walls to shift without doing damage to the overall structure. It was hard not to imagine the young boy waking up on a sunny morning and heading out to enjoy another day with his siblings and cousins, a day of hairbreadth escapes and fanciful adventures.

Uncle Quarles's farm was an important location for Mark Twain. More than once he would come to use it as a setting for episodes in his novels. He remembered that the "...farm has come [in] very handy to me in literature once or twice. In *Huck Finn* and *Tom Sawyer, Detective* I moved it down to Arkansas. It was all of six hundred miles, but it was no trouble...if the exigencies of literature required it" (5).

But both the farmhouse, and even the expansive landscape surrounding it, were only part of the importance of this locale to the development of the imagination of Sam Clemens. Equally significant were some of the people he came to know here, especially two slaves in whose cabins he was a frequent and eager guest. Aunt Hannah and Uncle Dan'l, in particular, were profound influences on

Sam. He would later acknowledge that he had used his memories of Uncle Dan'l's personality and kindness to create the character of Jim in *The Adventures of Huckleberry Finn*. But even more influential were the stories he heard these two tell. Their linguistic patterns made an enormous impact on Sam's ability to hear how their language could transport him to places far beyond even his most imaginative excursions around the acreage of the farm. In his autobiographical writings, Twain recalls vividly:

> *...the look of Uncle Dan'l's kitchen as it was on the privileged nights: when I was a child, and I can see the white and black children grouped on the hearth, with the firelight playing on their faces and the shadows flickering upon the walls...and I can hear Uncle Dan'l telling...immortal tales...and I can feel again the creepy joy which quivered through me when the time for the ghost story...was reached...for it was always the last story of the evening....* (18)

Twain never forgot these stories and the unique ways in which they had been told to the children gathered around the kitchen fire. He would write several books before he attempted to replicate the language just as he had heard it as a child on these memorable nights, but when he finally did so in *The Adventures of Huckleberry Finn*, American literature was forever changed. From that point on, the American language as it was actually spoken became a part of the repertory of every American writer.

For Mark Twain, Quarles farm was a place to which he would return repeatedly in his writings throughout the years. It provided him with memories of profound significance.

Hannibal, Missouri (1839-1853): "When I was a boy..."

Mark Twain's Boyhood Home in Hannibal, MO

In 1839 John Clemens moved his family some thirty miles east to Hannibal, a town with a much larger population than Florida, as well as having a ready access to the Mississippi River. He did so in hopes that this new location would provide him the opportunity to rescue his loved ones from the poverty and hardships they had experienced since their move to Missouri several years earlier. Ironically enough, however, it would not be the town of Hannibal that would rescue the Clemens family. Rather, it would be one particular member of that family who would ultimately rescue the town.

To anyone visiting Hannibal in the 21st century, two obvious truths make themselves readily apparent.

First, the town has gradually and modestly expanded westward, away from the riverfront. The usual combination of shopping areas, fast food franchises, and a variety of industries comprise the landscape of this modern portion of the town.

Second, the riverfront area and the center of the town's tourist trade is completely focused on the life and work of Mark Twain and, most specifically, on various locales identified in his novel, *The Adventures of Tom Sawyer*.

In fact, I do not believe there is another place anywhere in the United States that is so identifiable as the setting of a piece of great American literature than is Hannibal, Missouri. Almost everything in the riverfront area of Hannibal is connected in some way to that book.

Of immediate interest to visitors is Mark Twain's Boyhood Home, a structure carefully curated and presented to the public as the highlight of the riverfront area. It still looks remarkably like it did when Twain himself last visited it in 1902, and its rooms are filled with artifacts appropriate to the period when the Clemens lived here. But touring this home is much more than simply seeing a place where a famous writer wrote. In fact, Twain did not write *The Adventures of Tom Sawyer* here. He did, however, *experience* as a child living in this house many of the scenes he would later incorporate into his novel, and it is that sense of actually walking into the setting of the book that makes a visit here so memorable. "This must have been Tom Sawyer's room," you can almost hear someone saying. "And there's the window he'd climb out at night to meet his friend Huck Finn."

As visitors depart the boyhood home onto Hill Street, immediately across the way they see the Becky Thatcher house, home of Laura Hawkins, the girl on whom Twain based his leading female character in *The Adventures of Tom Sawyer*. This structure, like the boyhood home, has also been carefully preserved and opened to the public by the Mark Twain Boyhood Home and Museum as an educational center. Its rooms are not presented as they would have looked at the time of the setting of the novel, however, as Twain's narrative never included a detailed description of the interior of the Thatcher residence. But it is still quite easy for visitors to imagine Laura/Becky peering out her window at Sam Clemens's/Tom Sawyer's antics designed to amuse and impress her.

On the opposite side of the boyhood home, less than half a block to the northwest, the Blankenship dwelling has been carefully reconstructed on its original site. Tom Blankenship was Sam Clemens's boyhood friend whom Twain used as the model for his character Huckleberry Finn. Tom's father was also known, regrettably enough, as the town drunkard, as was Twain's depiction of him as the character "Pap" in the novel.

The proximity of these houses makes the characters and situations of *The Adventures of Tom Sawyer* seem to spring to life for the visitors to this place. How easy it would have been for Blankenship/Huck to come over to Sam's/Tom's window and call him down for nocturnal adventures on nearby Cardiff Hill which looms close by and forms the northern boundary of Hannibal.

On it, both in literature and in life, the boys would ramble in their midnight adventures. When the Clemens family lived here, this eminence was known as Holliday's Hill, after a family who owned property thereon. After the novel's publication and success, the town changed its name to Cardiff Hill as it had been identified in the book, so tourists could be assured they were in the right place while visiting this important setting.

About midway up its steep incline, and about a half mile west of the current stairway of 244 steps, there still exists the old Baptist cemetery where Tom and Huck in the novel oversaw Injun Joe commit a murder. I can still recall one of my students, a girl named Caitlin, walking through the rather unkempt grass with its ancient and tilted gravestones, and turning toward me and the other students as she exclaimed, "I feel like we have walked right into the book." Then she paused and added, "And I'm so glad we're not here at midnight with a dead cat in hand and a full moon out."

Everyone laughed, but I confess I thought how much Mark Twain would have enjoyed that comment.

Yet despite these lovingly preserved, reconstructed, and curated locations, for many of the visitors to Hannibal, its chief attraction lies about two miles south of Hill Street: the Mark Twain Cave.

This spectacular labyrinth of crisscrossing passageways would probably have been a draw for tourism even without being connected to Mark Twain, but the fact that the climactic moments of *The Adventures of Tom Sawyer* are set within its confusing net of interconnected rooms makes this cave a must-see experience. Add to this the fact that Clemens himself claimed to have been lost once in it, accompanied by Laura Hawkins, just as Tom and Becky were in the novel, and it makes this spot almost irresistibly interesting. (The fact that Laura Hawkins, in later years, denied having ever been lost here with Sam Clemens is inconsequential to the cave guides who actively point out spots where Tom and Becky would have experienced their moments of terror as they tried to find a way out, while eluding the murderous Injun Joe.)

The cave was designated as a National Natural Landmark by the U.S. National Park Service in 1972.

Yet even all this is not the full extent of Hannibal's offerings to tourists visiting the town. The Mark Twain Museum here includes interactive exhibits for all ages, first editions of Twain's works, original paintings and drawings by Norman Rockwell of his famous illustrations of *The Adventures of Tom Sawyer* and *The Adventures of Huckleberry Finn*, and many personal items which belonged to the Clemens family, including Twain's Oxford graduation robe which he wore when he was awarded an Honorary Doctorate from Oxford University in 1907.

There are also hour-long riverboat cruises on the Mississippi, and even Tom and Becky sightings for picture taking. (Middle School students in Hannibal compete annually for the opportunity to play the roles of Tom and Becky welcoming the disembarking passengers of steamboats mooring for a few hours to allow travelers to visit the town sites.)

And next to the Becky Thatcher house on Hill Street are both John Clemens's Law Office (moved here from its previous location closer to the river) and the Grants' Drug Store where the Clemens family lived on the second floor when their finances were at a low ebb.

These two structures figure in Twain's writings other than *The Adventures of Tom Sawyer*. In his travel narrative *A Tramp Abroad*, Twain interrupts his description of his travels to recount a memorable boyhood experience. One evening he had sneaked into his father's law office with the intention of spending the night there rather than running the risk of being punished at home. Although he tried to fall asleep, the moonlight streaming through the office window gradually revealed the arm of a dead man lying on the floor of the room. Sam hesitated as long as he could stand it, then he bolted out of a window and ran home, more terrified of that dead body than he was of any parental discipline that might be his due.

Just next to the Law Office is Grant's Drug Store, a location that earned a spot in *The Adventures of Huckleberry Finn*. While Sam was still a child living in the house on Hill Street, he witnessed a murder near the intersection of Hill and Main Streets, not very far from his home. A merchant named Owsley gunned down a man named Smarr who had been spreading slanderous stories about his business practices. Sam saw the body of Smarr moved into the drug store where the people trying to save him placed a Bible on his chest before he expired. Twain changed the names of the men and moved the action downriver to Arkansas, but it all happened right here in Hannibal.

Twain would leave this town of his youth and go on to travel widely. He found work as a "printers devil," and later fulfilled his boyhood dream of becoming a riverboat pilot. After the Civil War broke out and the steamship traffic ceased operations, he traveled west with his brother Orion to the mining towns of Nevada and ultimately began a career as a journalist. As such he visited the Sandwich Islands and later joined the passengers of the first pleasure cruise ever chartered across the Atlantic to Europe and the Holy Land. He became famous both as a speaker and as a writer, making his reputation as a humorous chronicler of the foibles and follies of the people he observed.

But he never forgot Hannibal. And when his humorous travel writing had begun to exhaust itself, Twain turned instead to the crafting of fiction. In casting his mind back to his childhood years spent in this small town on the western shore of the Mississippi, he discovered a vast treasure of actual and imagined exploits. His memories of Hannibal would inspire him throughout the entire course of his storied career.

The Mississippi River 1857-1861; 1882:
"...the bittersweet fruits of inevitable change"

By any account, the Mississippi River itself was another powerful influence on Mark Twain. It rolled past the Missouri hometown of his childhood and beckoned him to play in its often troubled and dangerous eddies. He and his friends sported there in their youth, and, as an adult, Twain fulfilled a childhood dream by managing to become a steamboat pilot, repeatedly traversing over a thousand miles of its waters from St. Louis to New Orleans and back again. In later years he mentioned that the river had brought to his acquaintance every character who had appeared in his fiction. And of course, the river itself played a central role in the tale of two of his most beloved characters, Huck Finn and Jim, the escaped slave, in *The Adventures of Huckleberry Finn*. Initially the river provides an open path to freedom for the two runaways. Then, after they miss their chance to head north on the Ohio, the Mississippi becomes a powerful force pulling them further south toward capture and slavery.

When Twain reached this pivotal moment while writing *The Adventures of Huckleberry Finn* in 1882, his inspiration ran dry, and he pigeonholed the manuscript, hoping to pick it up again at some future time. Although the narrative of *The Adventures of Huckleberry Finn* was temporarily stymied, Twain would soon begin to work on a new project, an effort that would ultimately result in a vivid account of his travels on the river: *Life on the Mississippi*. Often misunderstood, and seldom read in its entirety, this book explains more eloquently than anywhere else in Twain's writings the vital life lessons the Mississippi had taught him. Both the history of the composition of this book and the river's ultimate revelatory truth deserve to be appreciated.

It hadn't started out to be a book. Originally titled "Old Times on the Mississippi," Mark Twain crafted a series of articles for the prestigious *Atlantic Monthly* magazine, publication in which would testify to the height of one's standing in the loftiest circles of American intellectual respectability. These articles chronicled Twain's experiences while becoming a riverboat pilot in the years immediately prior to the outbreak of the Civil War. They were, by turns, informative insights into the world of steamboats and steamboat men (a world quickly becoming obsolete because of the ascendancy of railroads), humorous recollections of a boy's rite of passage into manhood, and a continued appreciation of American culture which Twain had first synthesized in the Missouri chapters of his first novel, *The Gilded Age*.

The success of the magazine articles logically led to the idea of a book, conceived at first as a sort of similar exercise to his earlier best sellers, *The Innocents Abroad* and *Roughing It*. Twain had produced these volumes by bringing together his previously published newspaper pieces, adding additional material when necessary, and fabricating these elements into the whole cloth of his signature literary genre: the humorous travel narrative.

Life on the Mississippi, however, would ultimately assume a much more serious tone. It stands as Mark Twain's acknowledgement of the fact of unavoidable and inevitable change. Reflecting the duality of his pen name, *Life on the Mississippi* is sometimes a playful remembrance of youthful folly and adventure. At other times its text is mingled with currents of deep melancholy. It would be Twain's most misunderstood masterpiece.

What frequently seems to lead readers astray may be linked to the book's structure. Darrel Abel's assessment is indicative of the typical critical response to the volume:

> ...the...book consists of two portions very different in their tone. The first twenty chapters, consisting mostly of the Atlantic articles, are a nostalgic evocation of pre-Civil War days of piloting on the river, and especially of Mark Twain's experiences as a cub pilot. The last forty chapters are a rather dry description of the lower river and the towns along it during the 1880's. (70)

Undoubtedly this assessment was further bolstered by the fact that Twain **had** taken a return trip to the river in 1882, traveling from St. Louis to New Orleans and then from New Orleans north as far as the river was navigable by riverboat. Doing so gave him the opportunity to take notes that helped him increase the heft of his earlier magazine articles to subscription book size.

The *Atlantic* articles are used first, as Abel notes, and the record of the later river voyages follows in roughly chronological order. It would appear, then, that *Life on the Mississippi* was little more than a none-too-expertly patched together literary quilt of river remembrances past and present. But a closer reading reveals a much more consistent, and pensively beautiful, organizational scheme. The entire work revolves around a central human paradox: that a price must always be paid for progress. Change is an essential ingredient of all advancement. But it also carries with it an equal amount of melancholy.

This insight is a constant thread running through both halves of the manuscript, and it is a theme greater than any maudlin sense of a lost past (a theme that many scholars have argued to have found, particularly in the latter sections of *Life on the Mississippi*).

It is present from its earliest chapters when Twain describes his rapturous love affair with the river and the craft of piloting. He notes, in an often-quoted passage, "If I have seemed to love my subject [being a river pilot], it is no surprising thing, for I loved the profession far better than any I have followed since, and I took a measureless pride in it" (118). Twain's valuation of this career verges on hyperbole, coming as it does, from the pen of one of America's greatest men of letters. And he reiterates his feelings at the end of the first section of the book:

> *Time drifted smoothly and prosperously on, and I supposed—and hoped—that I was going to follow the river the rest of my days, and die at the wheel when my mission was ended. (185)*

Passages such as these are at the heart of evaluations like Abel's quoted above, responses that enjoy the book's "nostalgic" glances back at the antebellum river life of the mid-19th century. Yet such observations miss the greater point of Twain's recollections. His mastery of this beloved occupation was obtained at a considerable cost. Note Twain's assessment of the "price" he paid for "learning the river":

> *Now when I had mastered the language of this water, and had come to know every trifling feature that bordered the great river as familiarly as I knew the letters of the alphabet, I had made a valuable acquisition. But I had lost something, too. I had lost something which could never be restored to me while I lived...the romance and beauty were all gone from the river. All the value any feature of it had for me now was the amount of usefulness it could furnish toward compassing the safe piloting of a steamboat. (78, 80)*

Twain is not lamenting a past glory that can never come again, nor is he ruminating about a diminished present. He has apprenticed for a profession that he loved "far better than any I have followed since," but even this beloved profession has been learned at a cost. He no longer can see the beauty of the river that had bewitched him at an earlier time. The Mississippi has become something new, something very different: it has become the venue of a career on which passengers' lives depend.

And, as if to emphasize this point, Twain ends this "cub pilot" section of *Life on the Mississippi*, not with a triumphant valedictory glorification of the lost art of river piloting, but with a poignant account of his younger brother Henry's death, resulting from the explosion of the steamboat *Pennsylvania*'s boiler. Prior to Twain's experiences "learning the river" as a "cub" pilot, he had viewed the river "...in a speechless rapture" (79). His success in attaining his pilot's license had been the greatest acquisition of his young life. Yet hard upon his account of this grand achievement, Twain is brought face to face with a wrenching personal tragedy. He is forced to acknowledge that along with his newly earned privileges have come undreamt of potential liabilities

Henry had not been a passenger on Twain's steamboat when he met his untimely fate. Yet Henry's tragic end served to underscore Twain's understanding of the deadly earnestness of his new occupation. If pilots were not constantly mindful of their responsibilities, lives could be lost. The "rapture" and beauty of the Mississippi had been exchanged for professional knowledge. Twain sees this progress in a complex and ambivalent light. It illustrates, for him, the inevitable paradox: new perspectives inevitably obliterate older ways of seeing. The wisdom of age carries with it the dissolution of the wonder and beauty of naive and idealistic youth

This paradoxical theme recurs throughout the entirety of *Life on the Mississippi*, regardless of which half of the volume one is reading. In the second part of the work, for instance, which provides an account of Twain's more recent cruise down and up the Mississippi, he observes how piloting has become markedly easier in the years since he had last stood at the wheel:

> ...the national government has turned the Mississippi into a sort of two-thousand-mile torchlight procession. In the head of every crossing, and in the foot of every crossing, the government has set up a clear-burning lamp. (232)

Now there will be no more daring decisions for a pilot to make, hoping against hope to find the right channel in order not to risk ripping the bottom out of the boat. Now steamboats can proceed safely at all hours and in all weather conditions. And the cost? Twain continues:

> But this thing [placing the channel beacons] has knocked the romance out of piloting, to a large extent. It and some other things together have knocked all the romance out of it. (232)

Once again, Twain finds that progress has both blessed and blighted the profession that he so loved. The channel lights have made piloting much safer, but also much more pedestrian.

Such progress, such change, is not only a function of a man's conscious decision (such as Twain's decision to become a pilot); it is as inevitable as the changing channel of the river itself. From the earliest pages of *Life on the Mississippi*, readers have learned of the constantly shifting riverbed. Overnight, we are informed, a river town can find itself landlocked, while another location has now become prime real estate for a new port city, all because of a new cutoff, a new rerouting and shortening of the river. The Mississippi has taught him that all change works in a similar way, and he makes this case memorably in chapters 31 and 32 of the second half of his narrative.

These chapters purport to be simply a diversion. They contain a lurid tale of the murder of a man's wife and daughter by a renegade Union soldier during the last days of the Civil War. Twain confides this story to two fellow passengers who are traveling downriver with him, a story that was related to Twain by a dying man named Ritter, whom he had met in Germany a year earlier. Ritter had been the husband and father of the murder victims, and he had determined to revenge their deaths through use of the newly developed practice of fingerprint analysis. He had identified the killer, but in his haste to exact his revenge, he had unintentionally caused the death of an innocent man. This man, Ritter told Twain, had earlier hidden a treasure behind a foundation stone of the livery stable in Napoleon, Arkansas. But after his botched attempt to revenge his wife and child's murder, Ritter had fled the scene. Now, on his death bed, having learned that Twain would soon be traveling down the Mississippi, Ritter had begged him to stop at Napoleon, find the treasure, and send it to the impoverished son of the innocent man whose death Ritter had mistakenly occasioned years earlier.

At the conclusion of Twain's retelling of the story, the travelers debate whether or not they should dispose of the money as the dying Ritter had requested. After a lengthy argument, they decide that such a windfall would only be a curse to the son. It would, they agree, "...rot his principles, paralyze his industry, drag him to the rum shop, thence to the gutter, thence to the almshouse..." (283). And so, in the true spirit of Twainian altruism, the men decide that they will disembark at Napoleon, find the loot, and keep it for themselves. Yet change, being the inevitable agent that it is, has another trick up its sleeve. The river, once bordering the town of Napoleon, Arkansas, had shifted its course and now ran directly over the previous location of the town, carrying away both it and any hidden fortune it may once have contained.

Yet Twain wants his readers to see the story in a more profound light than simply as a parable about human greed (though it certainly is that). He closes the 32nd chapter with an arresting series of references:

> Yes, it was an astonishing thing to see the Mississippi rolling between unpeopled shores and straight over the spot where I used to see a good big self-complacent town twenty years ago...the town where we were handed the first printed news of the Pennsylvania's mournful disaster a quarter of a century ago; a town no more—swallowed up, vanished, gone to feed the fishes; nothing left but a fragment of a shanty and a crumbling brick chimney! (286)

Suddenly we are no longer in Germany, no longer even involved in a sensational tale of murder and revenge. It is Mark Twain, even Sam Clemens, who is speaking. He has known the town. This was the town where he had first heard of the steamship explosion that took the life of his beloved brother, Henry. And now, it is "a town no more." But this change in the river channel is not simply a cause for a lament for an irretrievable loss. In some ways, the shift in the river has brought about a few good results. The selfish motives of the treasure seekers have been thwarted; the scene of an unintentional crime has been erased. But, as always, at a cost. Napoleon, Arkansas, is gone forever.

In instance after instance, the episodes comprising *Life on the Mississippi* revert to the same paradoxical truth. Change brings both inevitable improvement and melancholy loss, opportunities for betterment and unavoidable regret. The tone of the book ultimately, then, is not one of nostalgia, for nostalgia implies a longing for the past, a better time. That is not what Twain sees on the Mississippi, neither in his youth nor twenty years later. What he sees, and what he recounts with great eloquence, are the bittersweet fruits of inevitable change. The river, like the man writing about it, is forever "twain" in its purposes and in its effects.

The Hartford House (1874-1895):
"the best game on earth"

Much had transpired in the life of Samuel Clemens since the periods when he had piloted steamboats on the Mississippi, mined for silver in Nevada, and toured Europe and the Holy Lands. He had become an author. He had begun to attract large audiences as a lecturer. He had written an enormously popular humorous travel book. And, most importantly, in 1870, he had married Olivia Langdon, the second child of Jervis Langdon, one of the most prominent citizens of Elmira, New York. In 1871, Twain commissioned the building of this spectacular house in the fashionable Nook Farm section of Hartford, Connecticut.

Surely Twain must have realized that the woman with whom he had fallen in love "at first sight" was accustomed to a level of society and influence quite different from anything the Clemens family had ever experienced in Florida or Hannibal. And Sam's social standing in any of the subsequent locales in which he had lived had been no better. But now he was rising in both fortune and status, and he certainly wanted to give Lily every assurance that she had not allied herself poorly. If anything, he wanted to outdo and outshine the affluence into which she had been born. And just about every detail of the magnificent house on Farmington Street in Hartford seems designed specifically to attest to his efforts to do precisely that.

Carol and I have visited this home several times over the years. When I asked her what words came to her mind in thinking about this place, she immediately responded, "Sheer delight." Then she explained herself a bit more thoroughly by adding, "The whole house seemed to be constructed for the happiness of the family." Twain would have agreed. Indeed, he said so himself with great eloquence:

> To us, our house was not unsentient matter—it had a heart, and a soul, and eyes to see us with; and approvals, and solicitudes, and deep sympathies; it was of us, and we were in its confidence, and lived in its grace and in the peace of its benedictions.

The repeated word "us" in this description is particularly apt, for the entire home is unimaginable without an active, vital family in residence.

However, without a doubt, its architecture from the very start was also meant to impress. The expansive porch, the numerous gables and chimneys, the tower balconies, and the intricate brickwork all attest to the highest standards of taste and style of the well-known New York architect Edward Tuckerman Potter who completed the structure in 1874, the year the Clemens family moved in and settled here.

Still, it is important to note, as well, that much of the grandeur that dazzles today's visitors was the result of additions made to the home in 1881. By this time Clemens's fortunes had risen to the point where he was able to hire the Associated Artists, a firm of interior decorators whose members included Louis Comfort Tiffany, to further ornament the premises.

The first floor contains six rooms, each more spectacular than the last, where friends and guests dined, read, played instruments, and conversed for hours on end. Today docents tell stories of family gatherings and theatricals, elaborate dinner parties, and a parade of notable visitors who thoroughly enjoyed their hosts' generous hospitality.

The second floor rooms were dedicated to the family. Perhaps one of the most memorable highlights here is Sam and Livy's beautiful bed with its carved angels gracing the footboard which they used as a headboard. The Clemens children were allowed to remove the angels for play as long as they returned them before they went to their own beds to sleep.

Only on the third floor is there any hint of Mark Twain, the writer and lecturer whose success had made all this grandeur possible. Here, in his spacious study, Twain could write at a desk placed near an arched window and also, for the first time in his life, enjoy a game of billiards on his own table placed in the other half the room.

Guides inform visitors that the billiard table provided Twain with a place where he could spread his manuscripts and keep track of his pages as he produced them in rapid succession. And that is a sensible explanation of the purpose of this piece of furniture which might otherwise seem more of a distraction than an aid to his work.

Yet this billiard table would come to serve an even more important function in Mark Twain's life. Albert Bigelow Paine, Twain's first official biographer, makes the following statements regarding the third floor study:

> [Twain] took up his writing-quarters...in the billiard room, which, on the whole, he preferred to any other place, for it was a third-story remoteness, and he could knock the balls about for inspiration. The billiard room became his headquarters...Mark Twain always had a genuine passion for billiards. He was never tired of the game. He could play all night. He would stay till the last man gave out from sheer weariness; then he would go on knocking the balls about alone. (613-14)

Yet Paine had never personally spent time with Twain in the Hartford house. He only met him years later, in late 1905, and had become his biographer the following year. But no one on earth would ever come to know Mark Twain any better than he, and the game of billiards would play an essential role in building their relationship.

Paine began the colossal job of synthesizing the myriad memories, fabrications, and scraps of knowledge that his simultaneously charming and touchy subject heaped upon him during his almost daily visits to Twain's Manhattan residence at the corner of Fifth Avenue and Ninth Street. Very quickly, Paine had realized the enormity of the task before him. Granted, he had been chosen by Mark Twain himself, to tell the story of his many faceted life, but this distinction alone did not carry with it any guarantee of special insight or even sympathetic understanding between the two men. Paine realized that he needed to become a friend of the revered author, not merely a stenographer or a compiler of data. But how could he hope to bring this about? His own account provides the surprising answer:

> He [Twain] was twenty-six years my senior, and the discrepancy of experience and attainments was not measurable. With such conditions friendship must be a deliberate growth; something there must be to bridge the dividing gulf. Truth requires the confession that, in this case, the bridge took a very solid, material form, it being, in fact, nothing less than a billiard table...The disparity of ages no longer existed; other discrepancies no longer mattered. The pleasant land of play is a democracy where such things do not count. (1324, 1327)

Much of what Paine would come to learn about Mark Twain emerged during their epic billiard matches in Twain's Manhattan home, matches that often lasted for hours on end, a shared activity that required nothing more of either man than the desire to enjoy the other's company. Here Paine could listen to Mark Twain without self-consciousness. Indeed, the evenings Twain spent hunched over the numerous possibilities of the various shots before him seemed to evoke from him the very material that Paine, the biographer, was so eager to attain. He confesses openly the importance of these moments of apparent diversion:

> ...it [the game of billiards] drew from him [Twain] a thousand long-forgotten incidents; it invited a stream of picturesque comments and philosophies; it furnished the most intimate insight into his character. (1330)

Paine's desire to befriend Mark Twain and his need as a biographer to fully understand his subject had happily coincided in a single activity. It quickly became clear to the younger man that his road into a deeper appreciation of Mark Twain would result from nurturing in himself "a genuine passion for billiards." He did so willingly, and, as a consequence, learned to know Mark Twain and his many moods better, perhaps, than many who claimed a more longstanding acquaintance. Paine also realized that in this game, "the best game on earth" Mark Twain would call it, lay a key metaphor through which to better comprehend both the man and his art. The metaphor, of course, was the game of billiards itself.

Billiards is a game of angles, a game that requires its players to see a variety of possible shots and an almost unlimited number of possible results of each carom. Success only comes as a result of a series of ricochets, the cue ball often traveling in exactly the opposite direction from what will be its calculated stopping point. Billiards is a complex game, requiring both intellectual and physical skill. One must conceive the shot, an aspect of the game that requires both imagination and creativity, but then one must also be able to execute the shot precisely and accurately. Both conception and execution are important, and both are required to enable one to win.

Mark Twain liked winning, in both literature and life. As for his tenacity in billiards, Paine observed his demeanor minutely:

> ...he [Twain] was always not only human, but superhuman; not only a man, but superman. Nor does this term apply only to his psychology. In no other human being have I ever seen such physical endurance. I was comparatively a young man, and by no means an invalid; but many a time, far into the night, when I was ready to drop with exhaustion, he was still as fresh and buoyant and eager for the game as at the moment of beginning. He smoked and smoked continually, and followed the endless track around the billiard-table with the light step of youth. At three or four o'clock in the morning he would urge just one more game, and would taunt me for my weariness. (1328)

That Paine found Mark Twain's energy and stamina "superhuman" is all too understandable, and the fact that this man of seemingly endless vitality could not only play billiards into the wee hours of the morning, but could also smoke and pace continually while doing so, may even have been discouraging. Yet here Twain was illustrating more than a mere enthusiasm for a pastime. He was defining his approach to both life and his art, for Twain's unique style of humor often is executed with the same flair for caroms and ricochets that characterize the game of billiards. Take two of my favorite examples of his wit. I have divided each quotation with backslashes to indicate the caroms leading to the final conclusion.

There are basically two types of people./
People who accomplish things,/
and people who claim to have accomplished things./
The first group is less crowded.

Just as in billiards, what makes the shot ultimately successful are the caroms before the hit of the balls. The final hit is the culmination of the shot, or, in this case, the heart of the joke. What follows now is my very favorite piece of Twain's humor. A multi-carom shot ending with a marvelous laugh.

I was sorry to have my name mentioned/
as one of the great authors/
because they have a sad habit of dying off./
Chaucer is dead,/
Spenser is dead,/
so is Milton,/
so is Shakespeare,/
and I'm not feeling so well myself.

Seven caroms before the final hit. Pure genius from the pen of Mark Twain.

Twain lived voraciously, always ready for some new adventure, always experimenting with some new perspective. Paine recognized the connection between the beloved game and the larger, more important, matter of Twain's unique literary style. He suggests as much in an early assessment of Samuel Clemens' humor:

> ...it was not Mark Twain's habit to strive for humor. He saw facts <u>at curious angles and phrased them accordingly</u> [emphasis mine]. In Virginia City he mingled with the turmoil of the Comstock and set down what he saw and thought, in his native speech. The Comstock, ready to laugh, found delight in his expression and discovered a vast humor in his most earnest statements. (228)

Paine's observations suggest a vital fact if one is to understand Twain's literary style: both his comic perception and his uniquely American "voice" were the result of Mark Twain's ability to see "at curious angles." It is this same ability that one must employ in order to play billiards successfully.

I have cited two of the hundreds of examples of such instances of Twain's "knocking the balls about" to create his uniquely characteristic comic style, but one of his most brilliant examples of his billiard-like comedy, occurred as early as 1875, when he had recently begun to work in the third floor room in Hartford.

Twain was preparing his first book of short pieces in a volume that would be published as *Sketches, New and Old*. But suddenly he saw one of those "curious angles" that he so loved.

Twain's reputation as "the wild humorist of the Pacific slope" had first been established by a simple rustic tale of a con man duping a braggart, "The Celebrated Jumping Frog of Calaveras County." The "Jumping Frog" had already been widely published in a variety of newspapers and had even appeared as the featured tale of a small book of collected humorous pieces of his journalism, yet Twain wanted to incorporate the story into this first volume of short works that he himself was shepherding into print. But how to do this without mere redundancy? How could he present his famous story with a freshness that would both retain and extend its humor?

Twain worked on this problem in the "third-story remoteness" of his billiard room study in the Hartford house, and, ultimately, he was able, characteristically, to see a way to breathe new life into his famous "Jumping Frog."

As a premise for including the tale in the collection, Twain casts himself in the role of an author confronting the frustrating challenge of seeing his own work translated into another language. He informs his reader that a French literary critic has done him an injustice:

> ...he [the French critic] says my Jumping Frog is a funny story, but still he can't see why it should ever really convulse any one with laughter—and straightway proceeds to translate it into French in order to prove to his nation that there is nothing so very extravagantly funny about it. Just there is where my complaint originates. He has not translated it at all; he has simply mixed it all up; it is no more like the Jumping Frog when he gets through with it than I am like a meridian of longitude. (Sketches 16)

What a literary coup de theatre! In one short paragraph Twain engages his readers' sympathies as a wronged victim of French (no less!) sophisticated taste, reminds those same readers that the Jumping Frog story is to be understood as "extravagantly funny," and whets their appetite to read again the tale that has been so heartlessly misunderstood by its French translator. But Twain isn't finished; the humor he will manage to wring out of his retelling is just beginning.

After printing the "Jumping Frog" as it was originally written—of course any fair-minded reader would want this—Twain provides the French "translation." Doing so is a masterstroke. Twain knows that his average subscription book audience is unfamiliar with the French language. But he wants to point out, quite subtly, that part of the real charm of his tale is how it recreates American idiomatic speech. As he caroms his tale off the French version, he rebounds with an English translation of the French translation(!), and the resulting humor of this now thrice-told story is masterfully heightened:

> It there was one time here an individual known under the name of Jim Smiley; it was in the winter of '49, possibly well at the spring of '50, I no me recollect not exactly. This which me makes to believe that it was the one or the other, it is that I shall remember that the grand flume is not achieved when he arrives at the camp for the first time, but of all sides he was the man the most fond of to bet which one have seen, betting upon all that which is presented, when he could find an adversary; and when he not of it could not, he passed to the side opposed. [And so on.] (Sketches 27)

Of course, this ghastly translation of a translation is incoherent and awkward, but what it misses most importantly is the texture of the Western idiom, the language of the mining camps that Mark Twain had introduced into literature. He uses the occasion of the mistranslation to encourage his readers to appreciate, not only the tale as it originally appeared, but also the quality of its language that had served to heighten both its realism and its charm:

> ...well, there was a feller here once by the name of Jim Smiley, in the winter of '49—or maybe it was the spring of '50—I don't recollect exactly, somehow, though what makes me think it was one or the other is because I re-

> *member the big flume warn't finished when he first come to the camp; but anyway, he was the curiosest man about always betting on anything that turned up you ever see, if he could get anybody to bet on the other side; and if he couldn't he'd change sides. (Sketches 18)*

Readers have been given a new copy of the original "Jumping Frog" tale; they are allowed to sympathize with a beloved and "wronged" American author; they can ridicule French prejudice and rarified "taste;" and they are invited to appreciate anew Twain's acute ear for American "native speech." No wonder that Mark Twain loved such games of literary billiards. No one could "go on knocking the balls about" any better than he could.

Paine makes another observation about Twain's billiard play that also has profound significance when considering his unique literary style:

> *He liked to invent new games and new rules for old games, often inventing a rule on the spur of the moment to fit some particular shot or position on the table. It amused him highly to do this, to make the rule advantage his own play, and to pretend a deep indignation when his opponents disqualified his rulings and rode him down. (614)*

Here is a beautiful and surprisingly complete articulation of Mark Twain's approach to literature as well as to the game of billiards. His career as a writer had been launched by "new rules for old games." For instance, Americans traveling in Europe were supposed to be reverent, earnest, and deeply impressed by the antiquity and grandeur of the cultural superiority they found there. Mark Twain as narrator of his first travel book, *The Innocents Abroad*, was often impertinent, invariably comic, and refreshingly disinterested in mere piles of chipped rubble or faded oil paintings. By caroming off conventional expectations, Twain had created a new game at which he was temperamentally a past master: the satiric travel narrative.

Such stylistic innovations didn't stop with the creation of a genre, however. Twain was constantly inventing literary rules "on the spur of the moment to...advantage his own play." When Huckleberry Finn speaks, not through the acceptable medium of a cultivated third-person narrator, but in his own unpolished and unvarnished vernacular, and when he acts according to his own set of values rather than obeying the socially accepted moral code of his day, Twain is breaking several understood rules of literary propriety. Yet he is doing so to "advantage his own play." Twain wants his readers to get close to his roughhewn but lovable character so that his ultimate transformation will feel more genuine and be more affecting than if his readers were able to hold Huck at arm's length by means of an "appropriate" narrative voice or an "acceptable" moral code. The results of such literary sacrilege, however, were virtually a foregone conclusion. Twain's "opponents" were all too ready to see him "rode...down":

> ...Huck Finn's morality...caused the book to be excluded from the Concord library...The orthodox mental attitude of certain directors of juvenile literature could not condone Huck's looseness in the matter of statement and property rights... (Paine 797)

But they were playing Twain's own game unaware. He noted with "a deep indignation" their rejection of *Huckleberry Finn*, and then wrote his publisher, Charley Webster:

> The Committee of the Public Library of Concord, Mass., has given us a rattling tip-top puff which will go into every paper in the country. They have expelled Huck from their library as 'trash and suitable only for the slums.'

> That will sell 25,000 copies for us sure. (Ward and Duncan 123)

By the time published copies of The Adventures of Huckleberry Finn had arrived for distribution by the subscription publisher's agents, that figure had more than doubled to over 50,000 copies. To this day Huck remains one of Twain's most popular books with over 20 million copies sold.

Mark Twain and Albert Bigelow Paine playing "the best game on earth"

For both Albert Bigelow Paine and for Mark Twain, then, the game of billiards held an invaluable and complex meaning. For Paine, it became a "bridge" between the great man and his young biographer, a democratic "land of play" where they could meet, befriend each other, and form a bond that would benefit each man profoundly. For Mark Twain, billiards held an even more complex significance. Undoubtedly the luxury of being able to afford a room dedicated to nothing more consequential than a game would have appealed to the vanity of the boy from Hannibal who had ultimately become such a legendary success. The game itself would also have given him a respite from his labors and a place to unwind with friends. Perhaps, too, the game provided him a reminder of a larger, more central truth: that his success, his genius, his characteristic literary style had been billiards all along, played by his own rules with "superhuman" resolve. For him the game of billiards was an "Inspiration Point" that had begun in his study in Hartford and which he had taken with him to every residence he occupied thereafter. It was always "the best game on earth," a game of which he never tired.

Quarry Farm in Elmira, New York (1871-1899): "Youth"

Quarry Farm in Elmira, NY (Privately owned)

As full as life had been for the Clemens family in their palatial dwelling at 351 Farmington Avenue in Hartford, Connecticut, that location had one undeniable and unavoidable drawback: it was almost impossible for Twain to write there for extended periods of time, even in his beautiful third floor study/billiard room. There were simply too many parties (sometimes up to four dinner parties a week), too many visitors (again, sometimes friends and acquaintances staying for weeks on end), and too much family time, however precious it was for everyone. And the family was growing.

Ever since his boyhood in Hannibal, Clemens had enjoyed spending the summers at his Uncle Quarles's farm. And now Livy suggested that the family might enjoy vacationing during the summer months with her sister Susan Crane and her husband Theodore at their farm in the hills above Elmira, New York. It would relieve the Clemens of the social pressures of Hartford; it would provide Livy the support and assistance she required for her periods of pregnancy and childbearing; and it would give Sam the quiet time he needed to write the books that the family depended on to meet their ongoing expenses.

Even the names of the two summer destinations were oddly parallel: Quarles farm in Missouri and Quarry Farm in Elmira, New York. And once again Twain's imaginative powers would be profoundly stimulated by this time away from home.

I have often wondered what it would have been like to invite Mark Twain into one's home for a summer. I keep visualizing a cyclone entering the family parlor. Certainly, Twain's continuous cigar smoking was not welcome in the house. Furthermore, after only a summer or two, Theodore commissioned the construction of an octagonal study designed for the exclusive use of his energetic brother-in-law. It was built on the top of a hill about 100 yards west of the Crane's home. The site included a glorious view of the Chemung River valley, and nearby a stone stairway led down to the spacious porch of the main house.

The Clemens family would summer at Quarry Farm for eighteen years (1871-1889). Livy would give birth to all three of their daughters here, with Susan's faithful help. And here, Sam, happily ensconced in his literary pilothouse on top of the hill, would produce his greatest books.

My research had informed me that his study still existed, though not in its original setting near Quarry farm. It had been given to Elmira College in 1952. It had been installed on the college campus and was open to visitors. I had also learned that Elmira's Woodlawn Cemetery held the final resting places of both Livy and Samuel Clemens, together with their children, Langdon, Suzy, Jean, and Clara. Elmira, New York, then became a travel destination that was high on my list of places I wanted to visit, and in the summer of 2007, my wife, Carol, and I managed to do so.

Our first stop in town was the campus of Elmira College. I had learned that at this time of year it was advisable to call ahead for permission to visit the Twain study, and I had done so, setting an appropriate time. We arrived just as we had planned, and I followed the directions I had received to find the location of the study. It was easily recognizable as we walked toward it, and a young college woman was there awaiting our arrival.

Twain's Quarry Farm Study relocated to Elmira College

"Good afternoon," the young woman greeted Carol and me as we turned down the path to the site of the reconstructed study. "And welcome to Elmira College and to the place where Mark Twain wrote some of his most important books."

"Well," she continued, "not in its original location, but this is the very room where Twain worked when he created his famous characters Tom Sawyer, Huckleberry Finn, and Jim, among many others. I'm April, and I'd be happy to answer any questions you might have about this place."

Carol and I thanked her and proceeded up the steps and into the small study.

"Are you a student here at Elmira?" I asked our young guide.

"Yes," she answered.

"And are there many student visitors to this place?" April hesitated for a minute, and then she spoke out quite openly. "Not as many as I wish there were. It's an extraordinarily important spot for American literature, but most of the students take it for granted. I think it's because it's been here so long it's just part of the scenery to them."

I was taken by the candor of her answer, and I followed up with another question.

"Why was this structure brought to the campus in the first place?" I asked her.

"Because no one was caring for it after the Cranes left Quarry Farm. Trees had grown up around the hill, blocking its view of the countryside, and there had been some minor vandalism of the building. The owners of the property thought that this relocation would save the building, and it has done so, as you can see."

Indeed, the study looked very similar to the photographs I had seen with Twain sitting here, and I asked April if I could sit in one of the rocking chairs decorating the room.

"Absolutely," she smiled.

I couldn't resist asking her one more question. "April, do you enjoy reading Twain's books, and, if so, which one is your favorite?"

She nodded affirmatively, and then said, "My favorite is one that not too many people have ever read. It's *Joan of Arc*. It wasn't written here in this study, but I find it a very moving and important book. I wish more people would read it."

"That's a great answer," I responded immediately, "and Twain himself would have approved. It was his favorite as well, because he saw his precious daughter Susy as being very much like her."

Having the opportunity to see--and even to sit in--the actual octagonal study where Mark Twain had written *The Adventures of Tom Sawyer*, *The Prince and the Pauper*, *The Adventures of Huckleberry Finn*, and *A Connecticut Yankee in King Arthur's Court* was an experience never to be forgotten. Although this structure had been moved from its original location and had been transplanted here onto the grounds of Elmira College, it remains the crown jewel of the many places associated with the legacy of this great writer.

I had one last question for April before we left. "Can you tell us how to find Quarry Farm?"

"Yes," she answered, "but it's owned by Elmira College now and isn't open to visitors. The house is reserved for Twain scholars who can apply to stay there while they're working on their papers and books."

"I understand," I began, "but wouldn't it be possible to just get a quick picture of the farm? I'm a teacher, and I'd love to be able to show my students what it looked like."

April answered quickly, "I don't think that would be a problem," and then she gave us directions.

It had been wonderful seeing this octagonal study. Surely, in its original location, it would have qualified as Mark Twain's most famous setting. Here, transplanted to the grounds of Elmira College, it seemed more like a curious relic from an earlier age. Happily, however, it was guarded today by a welcoming young woman interested in keeping the memory of Twain's contribution to our literature gratifyingly alive.

After a brief stop at the nearby Woodlawn Cemetery to see the final resting places of Mark Twain, Livy, and their children, Carol and I proceeded up into the hills above Elmira in search of Quarry Farm.

April's directions turned out to be excellent. We soon pulled off the road into a driveway leading to the Quarry Farm house, but there was no way to get a decent picture of it from that direction. Carol was for turning around and accepting the fact that we wouldn't be able to photograph this location, but I saw a young man watering plants nearby. I quickly got out of the car and went up to him.

"Sorry to bother you," I began, "but we've come here from St. Louis, and I had hoped to get a picture of Quarry Farm. Would it be possible for me to do that without bothering anyone?"

The young fellow smiled at me as he answered. "Sure. Actually, there's nobody here right now. You can go out on the lawn there and get a good picture."

I thanked him, waved to Carol that it was okay, and ventured out onto the large grassy area below the house. I was able to get a beautiful picture of the farm from the south, looking up at the building and its expansive porch. By the time I had come back up to the driveway, Carol was standing outside our car, and I introduced her to the young man who had continued his watering.

I had another thought, so I decided to take a chance. "Could you indicate to me the spot where Mark Twain's octagonal study had been located?"

"Sure," he agreed, and pointed to a swath of mown lawn toward the west of the house. "If you follow that cleared area, it'll take you right up to the place where it used to be. There's not much to see up there, but you'll find the spot pretty easily."

"Thanks," I said, and then added, "Would it be possible for us to see the porch as well?"

He thought a moment. "You can't go into the house, but if it's just for a minute or two, I think it will be all right."

I motioned to Carol that I'd meet her on the porch and then went off to follow the mown pathway up the hill. In about a hundred yards or so, the mown area stopped, and I realized that I had reached the top of the hill. The octagonal foundation stones of what had been the location of the study were still quite visible, but the foliage around the site had so grown up that there was no view at all of the surrounding countryside. I paused for a moment, just thinking of the importance of this spot, and then started back down toward the house.

I can still remember the tangible thrill I felt as I noticed that, very close to the spot where I had begun my descent, there came into my sight the presence of an old stone staircase leading toward the farm. "I remember this," I found myself saying to myself as I made my way over to it. I had seen a picture of Twain descending these very stairs at the end of a day of work, holding a pile of manuscript pages he had produced and making his way to the porch where his family was awaiting his return. I had even seen pictures of the Clemens children sitting on these very steps anticipating the arrival of their father when he was writing *The Prince and the Pauper*, so that they could hear the latest installment of that wonderful tale. And now I was coming down, very carefully, this same set of stairs, and just beyond their base, the house came into clear view with Carol waiting for me on the porch.

I joined her and recounted my brief trip up the hill. There were several rockers on the porch, but as tempting as it was to sit down in one, I had no desire to make the gardener uneasy, so we gradually made our way back to the car. Before we left the porch, however, I looked out toward the valley below and realized that, although not quite as high as Twain would have been in his study, we were seeing essentially the same view. And, it suddenly occurred to me, what this view resembled was Missouri.

View from Porch at Quarry Farm near Elmira, NY

Green fields, rolling countryside, with a river gently wending its way through a verdant valley under a sunny sky--no wonder, settled up in his private octagonal study, Twain would have thought of Quarles Farm, of Hannibal, and of the Mississippi of his childhood. It was all here again for the taking, stimulating his imagination and memory. And with what gusto and genius he had taken it and created characters and stories that changed forever the course of American literature.

In the years to come, Twain and his family would leave off their annual visits to Quarry Farm. Their delightful practice of assembling on the porch to hear him read the product of his day's labors would recede into memory. Here he had reconnected with truths about himself that his lifelong wanderings may have hidden from him, but which his dear Livy knew all along. Her name for her husband, a man ten years her senior, provided the key both to his heart and to his greatness. She called him simply, "Youth." And there is evidence that Twain himself finally came to understand, appreciate, and accept Livy's pet name for him.

The Porch at Quarry Farm near Elmira, NY

In 1895 Twain faced financial ruin resulting from his terribly ill-fated investment in the Paige typesetter. In an effort to recoup the money needed to pay off his debilitating debts, he, accompanied by Livy, their daughter Clara, and Susan Crane, spent a year traveling the English-speaking world, while he gave an astonishing 140 public lectures. The tour ended in England in 1896 where Twain intended to write a book describing his experiences of the previous year.

He was weary and found his own state of health in decline, but his greatest shock was yet to come. The family received word that their daughter Susy had fallen ill, and only days later, the news arrived of her sudden and tragic death in the Hartford house she had loved since childhood. Twain would write in his autobiography, "It is one of the mysteries of our nature that a man, all unprepared, can receive a thunder-stroke like that and live" (423).

Yet live he must, and he still faced the need to write in order to repair his imperiled financial state. Twain crafted his last full-length subscription travel book *Following the Equator* in hopes that its profits, combined with the money he had made lecturing, would cover his accrued debt. It did so and more. The book's success was all Twain hoped it would be. Before his return to his country, he was able to pay all his debts in full and still have money on which the family could live.

But that book, I have come to believe, was much more than a relatively straightforward recounting of Twain's world lecture tour. *Following the Equator* also synthesizes many of the lessons Twain's full and productive life had come to teach him.

Of course, presuming to understand an author's intent is a very dangerous game. Such presumptions can so easily be wrong. And what is worse, there would appear to be no absolute way of proving one's conclusions to be correct, barring some miraculous find of a letter or journal written by the author identifying exactly his purpose for writing.

Perhaps so. Yet, from the very outset, this book feels autobiographical in a more important sense than any mere travel narrative. The question arises, are the parallels between Twain's tourist observations and the needs of his personal life simply accidental or are they intentional? It is impossible to say, yet Twain has left what appear to be fascinating clues to suggest a deeper meaning, a more heartfelt poignancy, in this, his last sustained work, than one might reasonably expect from the prospectus of an around the world lecture cruise.

For example, is it meaningless that in *Following the Equator*, "...Mark Twain makes no attempt to mask his identity as its narrator" whereas in his earlier travel volumes he had always done so (Rasmussen 145)? Is there no additional suggestive meaning in the fact that "More images of Twain himself appear in *Following the Equator* than in any of his other travel books..." (David and Sapirstein 24)?

And turning to the text itself, is it merely coincidental that the captain of Twain's outbound ship is a man "under a cloud" (1/4), just as was Twain, the famous writer who was facing the specter of personal bankruptcy? Is it nothing more than a coincidence that Twain describes the ship's purser as a man "full of life" and possessed of "a gay and capable tongue" (1/5), but who also suffers dreadful bouts of debilitating pain, unbeknownst to the passengers who thought they knew him? Twain's own physical condition seems eerily parallel, as he suffered repeatedly from painful carbuncles throughout his world tour, although to both his fellow passengers and certainly to his continuously overflowing audiences, he was visibly the glib, inspired, and apparently tireless "Mark Twain," the most famous of American authors and a lecturer of world renown.

And in yet another parallel to his own life, Twain describes a Canadian who he deems "the brightest passenger in the ship" (1/5). Yet this man's prospects have been severely limited because of his addiction to alcohol. Even though Twain himself was an addicted—and now impoverished—investor in get-rich-quick schemes, he diagnoses with admirable clarity this young man's need to address and correct his desire to drink instead of merely attempting to refrain from it. Yet he leaves his own addiction unmentioned and its cure undiagnosed. At the very least, then, Mark Twain finds himself traveling among social and emotional, if not strictly intellectual, peers as he begins to chronicle his journey across the Pacific.

None of Twain's fellow passengers have been identified closely enough to give very clear and objective information about the extent to which their actual lives reflected the descriptions of them provided by Twain in the opening chapters of *Following the Equator*, but their parallels to Twain's own life and problems presage what will become a fascinating synthesis of travel narrative and autobiographical insights as Twain moves around the globe, heading, he hopes, for an improvement both in his peace of mind and in his financial standing.

One instance of such an insight occurs as his ship nears Australia's port of Sydney. Twain chooses to recount the tale of the wreck of the *Duncan Dunbar*, a passenger ship whose fate, Twain reminds his readers, was "one of the most pathetic tragedies in the history of that pitiless ruffian, the sea" (1/91). Briefly, the story tells of a ship filled with young women traveling from England to be reunited with their families and their fiancés who had come to Australia before them. These women's ship had sailed all the way to Sydney harbor only to be shipwrecked within sight of land. Not a single woman survived.

Twain assures his readers that this grim story is "told to every stranger that passes the spot," that is, the spot of the shipwreck (1/92). But surely this tale held special significance to Twain who had begun to write *Following the Equator* in England after concluding his successful speaking tour, only to learn of the untimely death of his favorite daughter, Susy, just before she was to join the family in England as had been their plan. Emotionally Twain had to have felt a heart-wrenching kinship to those earlier families whose fondest hopes had been so cruelly dashed. And it is just these sorts of subterranean parallels with the deepest sorrows and concerns of Twain's private life that make *Following the Equator* such a compelling reading experience. One is always tempted to discover in an anecdote or in an observation more personal, more revealing, glimpses into the soul of their enigmatic author.

Indeed, it is hard, as Twain's ship passes the island of Tasmania, not to see a special relevance in his account of the history of the tragically displaced natives of that beautiful locale. He observes, in summarizing the fate of the Tasmanians, that "they pined for their lost home and their wild, free life" (1/248). But it was too late for them. Twain follows up with an especially moving conclusion:

> ...they repented that they had traded that heaven for this hell. They sat homesick on their alien crags, and day by day gazed out through their tears over the sea with unappeasable longing toward the hazy bulk which was the specter of what had been their paradise; one by one their hearts broke and they died. (1/248)

Twain had barely set foot on Tasmania, had met virtually no one from the island (excepting a museum curator and a host or two), and yet his eloquent lament about the native population is unparalleled in any other section of *Following the Equator*. Only in the context of Twain's own personal tragedies does this passage find a compelling explanation. Like the Tasmanian natives, Twain and his family had lost both their home (in Hartford, too expensive now to retain) and their "wild, free life." Surely at the age of sixty Twain must have often felt that he had traded the heavenly life of a beloved writer and adored husband and father for the relative "hell" of the lecture circuit, even if it constituted a way out of his financial miasma. The homesickness and tears ascribed to the now destitute Tasmanians clearly mirror Twain's repeated references to earlier moments in his more successful years, years he looked back upon with the same "unappeasable longing" he invests within the hearts of the Tasmanian exiles. No matter how widely afield he might travel, Twain seems never far removed from his own private torments.

Until India. Here, the shift of tone is palpable. From the almost persistent melancholy of many of Twain's observations about Australia, Tasmania, and New Zealand, the reader of *Following the Equator* now finds himself awash in movement and color. Typical is this first diary entry upon landing in India:

> *January 20. <u>Bombay</u>! A bewitching place, a bewildering place, an enchanting place—the Arabian Nights come again!...It is winter here, yet the weather is the divine weather of June, and the foliage is the fresh and heavenly foliage of June...and the juggler in his turban is there with his snakes and his magic; and all day long the cabs and the multitudinous varieties of costumes flock by. It does not seem as if one could ever get tired of watching this moving show, this shining and shifting spectacle....* (2/13-14)

What has happened to the Mark Twain of the earlier passages? Simply put, the country makes him feel young. Livy had always understood this key to an understanding of her mercurial husband's character. And in India, Twain had found a place where, quite literally, he could become again that boy from Hannibal who so inhabited his imagination and called forth the essence of what was best in his nature. Here in Bombay, Twain is able to trade the "winter" of his adult responsibilities and failures for an endless "June" of enchantment, an "Arabian Nights come again." Like his alter ego, Tom Sawyer, Twain revels in the prospect of stepping into a child's fantasy world of turbaned snake charmers and magic, yet India is no dream. And the fact of its actuality lifts Twain into a new realm of spirited buoyancy.

It is during his Indian travels, when commenting on the appalling practice of the outlawed society of serial murderers, called Thugs, that Twain identifies the essence of this country's allure to him:

> *...when I was a boy in the then remote and sparsely peopled Mississippi valley, vague tales and rumors of a mys-*

> terious body of professional murderers came wandering in from a country which was constructively as far from us as the constellations blinking in space—India; vague tales and rumors of a sect called Thugs, who waylaid travelers in lonely places and killed them for the contentment of a god whom they worshipped; tales which everybody liked to listen to and nobody believed...the source whence the Thug tales mainly came was a Government Report...not republished in America...I heard of this Report for the first time a day or two ago, and borrowed it. It is full of fascinations; and it turns those dim, dark fairy tales of my boyhood days into realities. (2/98-99)

For Twain, there are no more important words than those with which the above passage begins: "when I was a boy." This magical clause opens a world of adventure, of imagination, of endless possibilities in a perpetual summer atmosphere. But now for Twain, India is no longer a land farther than the stars. He has traveled there, and India has reawakened in him the lurid fascinations of his childhood, even giving them the modern sanction and veracity of a "Government Report"! In short, his childhood fantasies, those "dim, dark fairy tales of [his] boyhood," have become the "realities" of his waking travels.

The effect on Twain is a profound rejuvenation of spirit and insight. As his writing about India proceeds, Twain's wit soars and his incisive observations about what he sees reflect the same freshness and humor that had characterized his earliest literary success, *The Innocents Abroad*. He pokes fun at the superstitious requirements of the Hindu religion. ("The Hindu has a childish and unreasoning aversion to being turned into an ass. It is hard to tell why. One could properly expect an ass to have an aversion to being turned into a Hindu" (2/171). Yet he still has the ability to laugh at himself:

Two [monkeys] came into my room in the early morning...and when I woke one of them was before the glass brushing his hair, and the other one had my note-book, and was reading a page of humorous notes and crying. I did not mind the one with the hair-brush, but the conduct of the other one hurt me; it hurts me yet. (2/263)

Most significantly, he begins to revel in "tall tales"--"...I had my first tiger-hunt. I killed thirteen" (2/210) and to enjoy with childlike rapture the experiences of riding an elephant and sledding thirty-five miles down a railway track in a handcar equipped only with a braking device--"...the most enjoyable day I have spent in the earth" (2/222). Here in India, Samuel Clemens, Mark Twain, and Tom Sawyer meld into one rapturous being, one "Youth" enjoying an endless procession of color, newness, and adventure.

This is what makes the India section of *Following the Equator* such a delight. It must have been a delight even for Mark Twain, the impoverished writer, for, although he spent equal amounts of time in Australia, India, and South Africa, the India section of his remembrance takes up nearly half of the book.

Of course, neither childhood nor youthful fantasies can last forever. One must return home to the responsibilities and exigencies of real life. But for Twain, this trip to India seems to have been a psychological respite far more important than a mere lecture tour would suggest.

The final chapters of *Following the Equator* constitute little more than a somber coda. Whether or not Twain consciously felt the inevitability of returning to the realities of his life's challenges and demands, there is a subtle hint of melancholy in the superficially cheerful tone with which he describes his ship's passage across the Indian Ocean en route to his next stop in South Africa:

> *This sort of sea-life is charged with an indestructible charm. There is no weariness, no fatigue, no worry, no responsibility, no work, no depression of spirits...If I had my way I would sail on forever and never go to live on the solid ground again. (2/290-1)*

It is significant that the "charm" Twain sees in this life at sea is simply the negative charm of an absence of all the troubles, the unpleasant realism of the "solid ground," that had necessitated his tour in the first place: weariness, fatigue, worry, and responsibility.

As he tours South Africa, Twain will once again find himself confronted with the political intrigues of Europe (specifically the continuing conflicts between the Boer and British constituencies) and the corruption of late 19th century colonial exploitation, personified in the figure of Cecil Rhodes.

Rhodes had already appeared in *Following the Equator*. He had been the subject of an Australian "tall tale" of a young man who cleverly gained a fortune from reading a newspaper article inadvertently swallowed by a shark. Now, however, Rhodes becomes Twain's chief target of venom. Why? Among other reasons, because of his wealth. The illusive dream of comfortable affluence has returned to beleaguer Twain, the indigent lecturer. His envy of the success of this giant of British enterprise is unmistakable:

> *What is the secret of [Rhodes'] formidable supremacy? One says it is his prodigious wealth—a wealth whose drippings in salaries and in other ways support multitudes and make them his interested and loyal vas-*

> sals;...an Archangel with wings to half the world, Satan with a tail to the other half. I admire him, I frankly confess it; and when his time comes I shall buy a piece of the rope for a keepsake. (2/376,378)

Twain has come to the bitter conclusion that only the corrupt prosper, and Rhodes would appear to be a perfect example on which to found such dour musings. This man of "prodigious wealth," who was nonetheless guilty of innumerable political and personal failings--"He has done everything he could think of to pull himself down to the ground; he has done more than enough to pull sixteen common-run great men down" (2/377)--had continued to be lionized by many throughout the British Empire. Twain, whose largest failings seem to have been making injudicious investments, was still, at age sixty, having to sing (or lecture) for his supper.

And just as the passengers on Twain's outbound ship had appeared to reflect the beloved writer's personality and difficulties, his fellow passengers on the final leg of his travels once again mirror Twain's outlook. He describes them as "tired" and "fagged out," and now he clearly includes himself in their number--"I seemed to have been lecturing a thousand years..." (2/381).

Nevertheless, by his journey's end, he had succeeded in his quest. The globe had been circumnavigated. A hundred and forty lectures were delivered in more than fifty different cities. He had gathered enough material to write *Following the Equator*, a book which, by January of 1898, would sell over thirty thousand copies, netting a profit that, combined with the net gain from the lecture tour, allowed Twain to retire his entire debt with a comfortable sum of $13,000 left over (Kaplan 350).

But, as the Mississippi had taught him years earlier, this newfound prosperity would come at a cost. Livy's health was never the same after the tour. The family would never again live in their beautiful Hartford home, now forever tainted with the memory of Susy's untimely death there. Twain would ultimately lose both Livy and their youngest child, Jean, in his remaining years. And he would never again write a book as substantial as *Following the Equator*.

But his humor remained to the end, caroming from one object to another. And, most importantly, he retained a love for and appreciation of that one quality with which the love of his life had always associated him. Whenever he would cast his mind back over his world travels, the memory of one country would invariably lift his spirits: India.

Its color, its vitality, its beauty were constant inspirations. It was, he observed in his autobiographical remembrances, "...the only foreign land I ever daydream about or deeply long to see again" (378). Perhaps this was because it had also been in India that he had managed to recapture the very essence of his nature: the "Youth" that Livy so loved in--and as--him. It was the land in which Sam Clemens, together with his alter ego, Tom Sawyer, were eternally riding elephants and lassoing tigers in an endless summer of their fondest childhood dreams.

10

Ernest Hemingway

"Print the Legend"

Ernest Hemingway's Home in Key West, Florida

Ernest Hemingway may well be the Pablo Picasso of 20th century American fiction. As was the case with Picasso, Hemingway's private life was an unsavory blend of egotism and amorality. But these two men's similarities also extend to their creative endeavors.

Like Picasso, whose experiments changed the direction of the visual arts of Europe in the 20th century, Hemingway's uniquely identifiable diction defined in significant ways the direction of American literary style during the same period of history. Like Picasso, Hemingway's admirers have been legion, and, again like Picasso, whose reputation towers over the other European artists of his time, the name Hemingway is much better known to most American readers than the names of many of his literary contemporaries.

And the parallels do not end here. Picasso, despite his numerous references to a myriad of wide-ranging artistic influences, extending from Egyptian wall painting and the history of Western Art to African tribal masks, seems in many ways to distrust the very medium in which he is working. His art rejects the beauty of visual illusion, preferring to peel back the layers of his subject matter in bold and often grotesquely powerful images. He simplifies in order to make his viewers see.

Hemingway's literary style creates a strikingly similar effect. Like Picasso, Hemingway seems to distrust his own medium of expression. Language, its elegance and its potential for sensuous beauty, is banished in a prose style devoid of embellishment or intricacy. Language is stripped of its eloquence for the sake of being "true." In some cases the truth it presents can have an almost haiku like simplicity, as in the struggles of Old Santiago in *The Old Man and the Sea*. At other times it lapses into inarticulate agony, as in the dying words of Harry Morgan in *To Have and Have Not*: "Ain't got no hasn't got any can't really isn't any way out" (224). In either case, the truth with which Hemingway leaves his readers is invariably one of loss, helplessness, and inevitable, yet somehow strangely triumphant, defeat. The Hemingway hero achieves his stature largely by his willingness to endure, never by actually prevailing. Santiago catches his fish, but then sees it torn from him by sharks. Jake Barnes in *The Sun Also Rises* finds love but is unable to consummate his desire.

"You are all a lost generation," Gertrude Stein observed of the artists and writers living in Paris at the time when both Picasso and Hemingway resided there. And both men reflect this sense of uncertainty and emptiness in their art. I wondered what Carol and I would discover as we traveled to visit the home in which Hemingway had lived and written several of the stories and novels for which he had become famous. What we found was Key West.

Key West is a curious combination of affluence and destitution, both a frayed end of the continental United States and a paradise for the tourist trade.

On the day of Carol's and my visit, our ship pulled into port, passing a multitude of newly built condominiums and high-end tourist venues catering to wealthy vacationers and to a mixed bag of celebrants from cruise ships. Yet once we were walking around the town proper, we saw, slouching on the steps of a store we passed, a collection of drifters and homeless vagabonds worthy of the photographic eye of Dorothea Lange.

Our first stop was not a residence but a bar, the most famous watering hole in the Florida Keys: Sloppy Joe's. And here the Hemingway myth began to rise before us, warping reality in a way that we would see played out on several occasions throughout our visit here in January 2017.

Sloppy Joe's is a cavernous tourist venue serving a large lunch and dinner menu, together with an impressively diverse selection of alcoholic beverages displayed on what it touts as the longest bar top in Key West. Local legend insists this place had been Ernest Hemingway's favorite tavern, and, as if to prove it, the decorative décor of this gymnasium-sized eatery is resplendent with all things associated with Key West's most famous literary celebrity. On display are over two dozen framed photographs of "Papa" at various moments of his career, even one image of him warmly shaking hands with a youthful, smiling Fidel Castro. Mounted on the wall over these images is a large swordfish and, a bit to the left, hangs an oil painting of Hemingway's fishing boat, the Pilar. Finally, an oversized blown up photograph of a *Life* magazine cover featuring Hemingway's ruggedly handsome face is placed in a spot overseeing the end of the bar.

On the far side of this large dining area is a small room over the door of which is an illuminated sign with neon blue letters reading "Sloppy Joe's Mercantile." This space is devoted exclusively to the sale of a wide variety of tee shirts, baseball hats, and other items of interest to tourists, many bearing the image of Hemingway. Guests are assured that the famous writer had indeed patronized this bar and that it had been in the same location for over sixty years.

All this is true, and yet not completely the whole truth. In fact, the bar Ernest Hemingway had patronized for the majority of the time he lived in Key West, Joe Russell's, "Sloppy Joes," was located a block or so down Greene Street and had been a much more modest venue. It still does business as "Captain Tony's," and bears a sign on its side wall identifying it as the building in which Joe Russell had run his "Sloppy Joe's Bar" from 1933-1937, the most productive years of Hemingway's literary life in Key West.

Russell moved his tavern to its current location in 1937, the result of a dispute with his landlord. When Hemingway had returned to Key West in 1938, he had willingly moved to the new setting run by this old friend, but the bar of the legendary drinking bouts was not the current "Sloppy Joe's" that tourists visit today. Does it matter? Probably not. The new setting is larger, more open, and is centrally located on the corner of Greene and Duval Streets. Needless to say, it is also surely more thematically devoted to the perpetuation of the Hemingway myth than the bar's earlier location had ever been. For Carol and me, this site was an excellent preamble to what we would experience next as we visited the Hemingway home on Whitehead Street.

We arrived there after lunch in the early afternoon. The house was quite busy with tourists both entering and leaving the premises, and after we had paid our admission fee, our docent, an amiable young man who I will name Steve, advised us to stay close to the front of the home so as not to miss the beginning of his tour.

I took a moment to stroll the grounds of the front lawn and took a picture from the spot Steve had recommended to me as the most ideal place from which to photograph the residence. Especially in comparison to the other examples of old Key West architecture we had seen around town, this building was impressively large. Arched windows on both the first and second floor looked out on piazzas that ringed the building. The whole picture was one of gentility and affluence, a lovely setting for the residence of a successful and admired man of letters. In just a moment or two, Steve called for his tour group to congregate around the front door, and we all entered, turning immediately right into a spacious front parlor.

The high ceilings, six arched windows, and pale blue walls all helped to give the room a wonderfully airy and pleasant feel. And as soon as we all had stepped in, Steve launched into his presentation.

"This house is one of the oldest residences in Key West, built in 1851 by Asa Tift, a successful maritime salvager and designer of iron clad warships." Steve further noted the home's most extraordinary feature: a basement cut into the coral rock underlying the house, an almost unheard-of luxury in Floridian architecture.

Steve then identified himself, although it was a relatively unnecessary gesture on his part, as a "major fan" of Ernest Hemingway's writing, mentioning several of the books he had worked on while living here in Key West: A *Farewell to Arms*, *The Green Hills of Africa*, *To Have and Have Not*, *Death in the Afternoon*, *For Whom the Bell Tolls*, as well as many of his most famous short stories. Steve then brought us together before a painting on the wall picturing Hemingway on the left, his fishing boat, the Pilar, in the center, and another less familiar man on the right.

"Do any of you recognize this fellow?" he asked us. As no one responded to his question, Steve continued, "That is Gregorio Fuentes, a longtime resident and fisherman who sailed with Hemingway for over 20 years." Steve looked around to let this bit of information sink in with his attentive audience. "And he was the model for Old Santiago in *The Old Man and the Sea* for which Hemingway won the Pulitzer Prize in 1953." With that, everyone in our group wanted to get closer to this image, and Steve was happy to wait until we all had taken a moment to appreciate its significance. He then invited us to accompany him into the dining room, urging us all to notice the various photographs placed on the wall there.

The dining room was dominated by a large and rather massive rectangular table surrounded by six chairs. Steve's interest, however, was directed toward the pictures of four women displayed on the walls of the room: Hemingway's four wives. He identified them chronologically: Hadley, Pauline, Martha, and Mary, and then went on to describe their lives with Ernest. Steve punctuated the irony of the fact that Hadley had actually introduced her husband to Pauline while they all were living in Paris, but he made no further comment about Ernest's abandonment of his first wife and their son. After all, this was Hemingway, the ultimate man's man.

It was Pauline's wealthy Uncle Gus, Steve added, who had given this luxurious home to the couple as a wedding gift when they took up residence here in 1931. "Pretty phenomenal gift, wasn't' it?" Steve asked us all as we looked around this beautiful setting. But now my earlier research started to penetrate the skeins of the Hemingway myth that Steve was weaving before us.

Upon moving in here, Ernest had immediately set about making serviceable for his literary needs a workroom on the second floor of an old carriage house out back. The living quarters of the house itself, however, at least as described by one local historian, had numerous features requiring major repairs: "antique plumbing...crumbling plaster...rotted window frames, broken windows, and rain-warped doors" (McLendon 79). The repairs of all these problems had been left for Pauline to oversee.

Steve now moved on to wife number three, Martha Gellhorn, herself a very talented writer and newspaper reporter. Steve recounted how she had first met Hemingway one day in Sloppy Joe's while her family was vacationing in Key West in 1936. During the following year, both she and Ernest had traveled to Spain as war correspondents to cover the civil unrest raging there. It was at that period that they had begun an affair. They would ultimately marry and move to Cuba after Pauline divorced Hemingway in 1941. Steve commented that this third marriage was tempestuous from the very start, largely the result, he believed, of the fact that although they were both writers, Ernest and Martha were employed by different news organizations and thus were constantly competing with each other. After a long pause, Steve then spoke briefly of

Hemingway's fourth wife, Mary, who had stayed with him until his death in 1961.

The final subject matter Steve brought up in this room felt oddly, even somewhat comically, apropos.

"Before we go upstairs," he began, "I need to tell you about the cats. They are all descendants of the first Hemingway cat that lived here, a white polydactyl named Snow White. Ernest had heard that these cats brought good luck, and so he never complained about their breeding. There are 53 cats who live on the property currently." And without further ado, Steve led us up to the second floor to continue the tour.

The most significant stop here was the spacious bedroom located over the downstairs parlor. The room also had numerous full-length arched windows and was bathed in light. The center of the Hemingways' bed, actually two twin beds joined together by an elaborately carved headboard, was currently occupied by one of the aforementioned polydactyl descendants of Snow White. She evidenced no interest in moving, and Steve continued the tour without comment. "That beautiful headboard was purchased in Europe. It had been a gate in a Catholic mission Pauline and Ernest were visiting, and she fell in love with it." We all appreciated the humor implicit in its repurposing, and then we were led out onto the piazza to walk around the home's second story and then to descend another stairway leading to the back of the house.

Finally we arrived at the small patio area outside the carriage house, the second floor of which had been Hemingway's workroom. Steve pointed it out to us, noting that in the over eight years Hemingway had lived here, he had produced in that room about 70% of his total literary output. But to my surprise, Steve then informed us if we wanted to climb the narrow stairs to see the room we would need to return individually, as the iron stairs leading up to it would not accommodate a group as large as ours. Instead, Steve asked us to follow him to the nearby swimming pool.

"What you're looking at," Steve began as we stood close to the impressively large pool, "is Pauline Hemingway's revenge." He looked around at our assembled group and then resumed talking. "Ernest had run off with Martha Gellhorn, and Pauline was angry. You all probably know that Hemingway had always loved boxing. He had installed a boxing ring right here where you're seeing the pool now. By working out with a sparring partner in this ring, he was able to keep himself in shape. Well, with her husband now being openly disloyal, Pauline decided to replace the ring with this pool. It's 64 feet long, 24 feet wide, and 9 feet deep, and it cost her $20,000 to build—in 1937 dollars. When Ernest returned and found the pool instead of his practice ring, he was furious. And when she told him what the pool had cost, he fumed that he was already down to his last cent, and he reached into his pocket, pulled out a penny, and threw it at her before storming off. Next day," Steve continued, "when the patio concrete was being set, she took the penny he had pitched at her and planted it in the wet cement. It's right where you're standing now." He pointed to a spot near our feet, and there indeed was an old penny encased in cement.

"I love that story," Steve said. "Go, Pauline!"

It *was* a great story, a tale worthy of a larger than life couple. But was it true? The penny was real, but my subsequent research has discovered a different local story that insisted the pool, rather than being Pauline's act of vengeance, had been her last-ditch effort to save her marriage. It is generally acknowledged that Hemingway enjoyed swimming in this pool every morning before his afternoon sojourns at Sloppy Joe's, and this version of the tale states that Hemingway himself had placed the penny as a humorous gesture to indicate how much the pool had cost, taking him down to his "last red cent." (But just for the sake of accuracy, there are others who insist that the pool had probably been financed by the same uncle who had given the couple the house in the first place.)

Steve then continued the tour by speaking about his theory as to why Hemingway had come to take his own life in later years, but here he lost me. I wandered back over to the carriage house and climbed the stairs to take a look at Hemingway's study.

I had to admit that Steve had been correct. Our tour group never would have fit on the metal stairway leading up to the second floor. And it was difficult to have more than one or two people squeezed into the narrow space inside the study that had been cordoned off for visitors interested in climbing up the stairs to look inside.

The room was quite large and was appointed ideally as a work space for a great writer. Between the windows on either side of the room were bookcases filled both with worn volumes and bric-a-brac. Above the bookshelves and elsewhere around the room animal heads hung mounted on the wall, attesting to the prowess of Hemingway, the big game hunter. A cat was curled up on one of three chairs, and a vintage typewriter was positioned on a round table that occupied the center of the room. Light poured into the room through the windows in the side walls and the two French doors on the wall opposite the entry. It was perfect, a tranquil haven, a fit setting for one of the greatest of American novelists. But I had to question the image it projected. This study felt more like a model vision than the hot, stuffy reality that had made it virtually impossible for Hemingway to want to work here much past ten in the morning. And I enjoyed reading another description of this room forwarded by a local historian of Hemingway's residency in Key West:

Ernest furnished his workroom with a squat cigar-maker's wood-frame chair having a wide leather bottom and a narrow leather back piece, and a simple round table on which he worked out his handwritten manuscript pages...and boxes of bits of works-in-progress, together with artifacts from his days as a lieutenant in the Italian army...The entire room was littered with the copious notes he had assembled over the past few years on the spectacle of bullfighting, as well as several hundred photographs...the study resembled something like a "lightly organized waste paper can," Pauline observed.... (McLendon 80-81)

For Steve, and, to be fair, for perhaps most of the curious tourists who had interrupted their travels to spend an hour here, the world this home presents is a fascinating, gracious, welcoming, and impeccably ordered showplace. It befits the stature of the man whose literary works helped redirect American literature in the 20th century. But the boozy, sometimes violent, sometimes brilliant, sometimes "lost" man whose name this house bears continues to be something of an unsolved mystery even here.

Only the cats remain. They rule the property with regal languor and still drink fresh water from the urinal become drinking pool that Hemingway had installed in the garden, edged with aging Spanish tiles, a gift from a now forgotten friend. But whatever the cats know, they keep to themselves.

I found myself thinking of the ending of a film directed by the great John Ford, *The Man Who Shot Liberty Valance*. In it a respected man who has risen to great political prominence finally reveals to a reporter the truth about an episode that had begun his ascendancy to power. After hearing the tale, the reporter crumples up his notes. When asked why he will not write the story, the reporter's answer is telling: "This is the West, sir. When the legend becomes fact, print the legend." Here in the most western of the Florida Keys, they still do.

11

Margaret Mitchell

The High Price of Charm

Margaret Mitchell's "The Dump" in Atlanta, Georgia

I love a great opening. And I am not talking simply about a "hook." Not the "He found his hand instinctively reaching for the butt of his revolver as he looked down the steadily darkening street" kind of opening sentence. Of course there is nothing implicitly wrong with such a beginning. A reader is plunged immediately into a narrative and, hopefully, is gripped by the story to come. But this is not the kind of opening I'm talking about. I love finishing a book, and then going back to read again its first few lines. And when its opening words lead me to discover, sometimes to my amazement, that the author had in fact set up—perhaps even summarized—the entirety of the work to follow, it thrills me. Such openings are rare, and their very rarity may at least partially explain my love of them.

Joseph Conrad begins his great novel, *Lord Jim*, with such an opening. He first introduces his hero, Jim Lingard, with what appears to be a simple physical observation: "He was an inch, perhaps two, under six feet..." Yet as this masterwork unfolds, it becomes increasingly obvious that Conrad has summed up in under ten words the entire predicament of his main character. Jim repeatedly falls short, his aspirations of heroic achievement thwarted by his own limitations of character. He aspires to greatness, the "six feet" height of the ideal hero. But always is "an inch, perhaps two" short of demonstrating the moral and physical stature he dreams of personifying. It's to Conrad's credit that we still care about Jim's flawed career, still hope for his ultimate success. But the opening of the novel lets readers know its inevitable conclusion even before the tale is fully told.

I was sixty-seven years old before I read Margaret Mitchell's astonishingly great masterpiece *Gone with the Wind*. I say it to my shame, as it was always one of my mother's favorite books. I had seen the movie and had enjoyed it thoroughly. Wasn't that enough?

Forty years ago, my mother wrote a note on the end page of her copy of *Gone with the Wind*. I discovered it by chance, and it reminded me of both her scholarship and her humble willingness to rethink any of her earlier assessments:

> *I have just re-read this absorbing, vivid account of our beloved South. I read it first in 1936 when MM wrote, or rather published, it. At that time I was so bewitched with Scarlett and Rhett that the depth—the woof and warp—of the book escaped me. This second reading was done slowly with conscious appreciation for that thorough historical framework, and I have enjoyed it immensely. I saw the movie six times. This second re-reading of the book brings to light the many interesting details left out of the film. No movie substitutes for a profound reading experience!*

And so I finally read *Gone with the Wind* "slowly with conscious appreciation" as my mother would have liked. And what I discovered was another great opening. Of course, I didn't recognize it as such immediately. It is impossible to appreciate the greatness of a work's opening until after one has had the experience of reading the book. Yet when I had done so, a fascinating fact came to my mind, a fact which docents at the Margaret Mitchell home in downtown Atlanta tell visitors touring the property. Mitchell wrote the first chapter of her novel last. In other words, she understood completely where her epic work was headed and what had been the lessons it had taught her along the way. The book was already written. She knew exactly how to open her story, though many of her readers, even today, miss her central point.

She begins with a straightforward observation and then adds to it a most consequential truth: "Scarlett O'Hara was not beautiful, but men seldom realized it when caught by her charm...." Fifteen words at the beginning of a novel of well over a thousand pages. But they perfectly presage the profound and ultimately tragic truth contained in this work. It is charm that acts like an opiate throughout the pages of *Gone with the Wind*. It is charm that attracts, that addicts, and that finally devastates every character it touches. And it is also charm that destroys the South, first, with impossible expectations of unachievable military glory and, later, with agonizing memories of an ideal past now hopelessly "gone with the wind."

Webster's offers a very helpful definition of the word "charm": "a trait or quality that fascinates and allures, as if by a spell, *to love, admiration, or submission.*" [my emphasis] And indeed the major characters of the book all seem to fall clearly within the boundaries mentioned here. All of them are "charmed," "as if by a spell" with a variety of dreams upon which they base their lives.

Ashley Wilkes is "caught" (to use Mitchell's perceptively descriptive word in her opening) by the charm of the genteel South. He describes its spell to Scarlett midway through the novel:

> *I do mind, very much, the loss of the beauty of the old life I loved. Scarlett, before the war, life was beautiful. There was a glamor to it, a perfection and a completeness and a symmetry to it like Grecian art...I belonged in that life. I was a part of it. And now it is gone and I am out of place in this new life, and I am afraid.* (735)

Afraid, perhaps, but also virtually useless. Ashley tries to split logs and plant crops, but he is hopelessly inept at such tasks. Later in the novel he is equally ineffective as a manager of a mill. His problem, as Scarlett diagnoses it, is that "He can't look forward any more. He can't see the present, he fears the future, and so he looks back" (1290). Rhett Butler, as is his wont, passes his verdict on Ashley more heartlessly but still accurately nonetheless:

> *I pity him because he ought to be dead but he isn't. And I have a contempt for him because he doesn't know what to do with himself now that his world is gone.* (1074)

What is particularly compelling about Mitchell's characters, however, is that they invariably become conscious of the "charm" that has seduced them. Ashley himself states clearly the problem he faces: "...we will never get back to the old times. And I belong to those old times...I do not know what the future will bring, but it cannot be as beautiful or as satisfying as the past" (294). For Ashley the charm of the antebellum South has led him to a submission more powerful than the Confederacy's loss of the war. His spirit is broken, and what is worse, he knows and accepts it.

Scarlett would appear to be a different case entirely. She adapts quickly to the changed world, plotting and pitilessly manipulating it in order to achieve her desired ends. But she, too, is a victim of charm, "caught" in its spell. In her case, however, it is not Ashley's "old times" of the antebellum South that has seduced her. It is the charm of Ashley himself. It leads her into an undying desire for and admiration of him that underpins almost every decision she makes. Of course, Scarlett would not call her deep feeling for Ashley "admiration." She would call it love, yet even she finally comes to realize that the figure for whom she has sacrificed so much and for whom she has conspired so tirelessly is only an image of her own creation:

> *I loved something I made up...I made a pretty suit of clothes and fell in love with it. And when Ashley came riding along, so handsome, so different, I put that suit on him and made him wear it whether it fitted him or not. And I wouldn't see what he really was. I kept on loving the pretty clothes—and not him at all.* (1419)

Yet even with this clarity of vision, Scarlett remains caught by the spell of Ashley's charm. Toward the very end of the novel, as Rhett forces Scarlett to understand that he is leaving her, that he is tired of a chase that he can never win, she is reminded of her earlier meeting with Ashley in the orchard of Tara and the look of complete resignation she had seen on his face. She observes that "...there was the same look in Rhett's eyes that had been in Ashley's eyes that day," and aloud she remembers what "...Ashley said once, about the old days." Rhett shrugs and, totally disconsolate, concludes, "Always Ashley." Moments later, and not giving "a damn," he walks out of her life (1444,1446).

For Rhett, too, had been "caught" by charm. In his case, however, it is neither the alluring charm of a lost past nor the addictive charm of an undying admiration that blinds its victim to reality. The charm, the spell, that bewitches Rhett is much more damaging. It is the curse of passionate, unrequited love. Even worse, Mitchell reveals to her readers that it is a curse about which Rhett has been helplessly aware almost from the beginning. If ever a character in a novel can be said to be intentionally self-deceived, and, as a result, self-destroyed, Rhett Butler is a prime example of this pitiable condition. Rhett himself best supplies his own description of his plight. He has been both fascinated and allured by Scarlett's charm from the moment he first saw her at Twelve Oaks. And the result has been devastating for him:

> *Did it ever occur to you that I loved you as much as a man can love a woman? Loved you for years before I finally got you? During the war I'd go away and try to forget you, but I couldn't and I always had to come back. After the war I risked arrest, just to come back and find you. I cared so much I believe I would have killed Frank Kennedy if he hadn't died when he did. I loved you but I couldn't let you know it. You're so brutal to those who love you, Scarlett. You take their love and hold it over their heads like a whip...But, fool that I was, I thought I could make you care.* (1437)

His dilemma, of course, is that he has found it to be impossible to make inroads into the charm of Ashley, a charm that has always spellbound Scarlett. He observes finally, and resignedly, "It seems we've been at cross purposes, doesn't it. But it doesn't matter now" (1439).

It finally *has* ceased to matter to Rhett because, at age forty-five, the charm that had held him captive for such a long time has finally been dispelled. His "tired eyes" see the terrible, ironic absurdity of his twelve-year long infatuation. He asks, "Scarlett, did it ever occur to you that even the most deathless love could wear out?" She cannot reply, and he answers his own question with heartless clarity:

> Mine wore out...against Ashley Wilkes and your insane obstinacy that makes you hold on like a bulldog to anything you think you want...Mine wore out. (1436)

And so the three main characters of *Gone with the Wind* end up devastated and alone. Ashley is widowed and only partially alive in a Georgia he no longer understands. Rhett is childless and worn out, mortally tired of pursuing an unattainable dream. And Scarlett has lost everything she ever pursued, except money. She may still believe that the charm she has wielded so expertly throughout the novel can change her fortunes once again--"Tomorrow, Tomorrow, I'll think of some way to get him back" (1448), but Margaret Mitchell offers no such assurance. Ashley, Rhett, and Scarlett have toiled completely in vain. All their lost causes *are* truly lost, permanently "gone with the wind."

And, as no one knew better than Margaret Mitchell herself, so was the South. The words she puts in Rhett's mouth at Twelve Oaks, early in the novel, speak lucidly of the suicidal charm of the South, a bewitching spell cast over its own people, blinding them to the inevitable consequences of secession:

> Has any of you gentlemen ever thought that there's not a cannon factory south of the Mason-Dixon Line? Or how few iron foundries there are in the South? Or woolen

> mills or cotton factories or tanneries? Have you thought that we would not have a single warship and that the Yankee fleet could bottle up our harbors in a week...I have seen many things that you all have not seen. The thousands of immigrants who'd be glad to fight for the Yankees for food and a few dollars, the factories, the foundries, the shipyards, the iron and coal mines—all the things we haven't got. Why, all we have is cotton and slaves and arrogance. (154-155)

In a similar vein, Ashley, upon his first return from the war, shows this contempt for the conflict engulfing his world:

> ...I see too clearly that we have been betrayed, betrayed by our arrogant Southern selves, believing that one of us could whip a dozen Yankees, believing that King Cotton could rule the world. Betrayed, too, by words and catch phrases, prejudices and hatreds coming from the mouths of those highly placed, those men whom we respected and revered.... (292-293)

Yet both Rhett and Ashley fight for the Confederacy. Even their clear understanding of the weakness of their military, social, and even moral position has not made them immune to the spell of the Southern cause. Of course, they fight for quite different reasons. Ashley for the honor he believes to be an essential part of the "old times" of the South of his past and Rhett in the hope that perhaps Scarlett will come to love him as a result of his willingness to fight for "the cause." But the destruction and devastation that occur as a result of the war are chronicled thoroughly in the second half of the novel.

In many ways, Margaret Mitchell was the perfect person to write it. Throughout her entire life, she had found herself at odds with the expectations placed upon her as a young woman of high social standing in the Southern upper class society of her day. In her early years, she had dressed as a boy, adopting the name of "Jimmy." Later, as a reluctant debutante, she had danced a Tango that so scandalized Atlanta that she was denied membership in the Junior League. Then after a disastrous early marriage to Red Upshaw, an alcoholic bootlegger, Mitchell again startled her family and social class by becoming a journalist in order to support herself independently. A year after her divorce from Upshaw, she married John Marsh, and rather than continuing to live in the stately Mitchell family home on 17th and Peachtree Street, she and her new husband moved to a place of their own, several blocks further west on Peachtree and closer to the center of town.

The building containing their small apartment still stands in Atlanta, surrounded now by gleaming glass international style skyscrapers. At the time when Mitchell and her husband lived here, it was a busy urban setting, full of storefronts, shops, restaurants, and grocery stores. Nothing was grand nor particularly glamorous. She called their residence "The Dump." And it was here, in a corner alcove area of their rather cramped front parlor of their first floor apartment, that she would write almost the entirety of *Gone with the Wind*. This place provides a particularly telling backdrop against which to understand just what it was that had fueled Mitchell's interest in characters like Scarlett O'Hara, Rhett Butler, and Ashley Wilkes, as well as in the epoch of Southern history surrounding them.

When Carol and I visited "The Dump" in late April of 2017, we immediately joined a tour group that had gathered in an antechamber, the walls of which were covered with information about Margaret Mitchell's life. Moments later, we were greeted by a cheerful young docent who I'll call Linda.

After welcoming us to the site, she began her remarks by informing us of Mitchell's early interest in storytelling and then went on to describe her schooling in nearby Washington Seminary, an all-girls school for the daughters of upper-class Atlanta families. Linda recounted Mitchell's experiences at Smith college, cut short by the death of her mother and Margaret's return to Atlanta to take on the responsibilities of being "the lady of the house," along with her maternal grandmother, with whom she found it hard to get along.

Linda's narrative then moved on to Mitchell's first unhappy marriage to Red Upshaw, her decision to become a journalist, her divorce from Upshaw, and, on July 4, 1925, her second, and much happier, marriage to John Marsh.

Linda then moved on to the story of Mitchell's recurring ankle injury which had forced her to forego her career in journalism and had left her temporarily an invalid, spending her time reading alone in "The Dump." And finally, Linda arrived at the day in 1926 when John had returned home from work, bringing with him a typewriter, a ream of paper, and a challenge for his wife to curtail her omnivorous consumption of every book in the nearby Atlanta library, and instead to become a writer herself. "The rest, of course," Linda concluded, "is history." And with that she led us onto the back porch of the Mitchell apartment and into its very modest kitchen.

One by one we stepped into this area which must have measured not much more than five feet square, and which then gave directly into the apartment's one bedroom. It was immediately clear to all of us why Mitchell had named these living quarters "The Dump." The kitchen held only a minuscule stove and a very limited pantry. Yet Linda assured us that, although small (its bathroom just off the hall was roughly the size of the kitchen), this apartment was the largest in the building. The other nine units all had shared kitchens and bathrooms. Linda wanted us to understand that for Margaret and John, "The Dump" had been an affectionate name, chosen in jest.

The bedroom was a larger room, perhaps 14 or 15 feet square, with room enough for a vanity, a large chest of drawers, a nightstand, a double bed, and, huddled against the outside wall, a plain white wooden table with two chairs. "This was their dining room as well as the bedroom," Linda remarked briefly, and then she made her way down the short hall, past the bathroom, and into the largest room in the apartment: the front parlor.

This room, with its two sofas and window seat alcove, allowed Linda to tell the stories she most enjoyed about Margaret Mitchell. We learned that after finishing each chapter of the novel, Mitchell would place it in a manila envelope and hide it somewhere in the apartment (under the bed, in closets, wherever she could find a space). She worried, Linda explained, that the Civil War setting and subject matter might offend the people of Atlanta, so she tried to keep her manuscript a secret from all but her most trusted friends. Linda went on to describe how Lois Cole, one of Mitchell's closest confidantes, had alerted her boss, Harold Latham, Editor-in-Chief of Macmillan Publishing Company, to the book her friend had written. At Cole's urging, Latham had come to Atlanta to meet the author, and Linda recounted with delight both the timidity and regret that had characterized Mitchell's final willingness to send Latham back to New York with so much manuscript that he had had to purchase an extra suitcase to hold it all.

Linda told a few more stories about the financial agreements Mitchell had come to make with both Macmillan and, later, with Selznick Studios, and then she opened up for questions.

I was standing near a small rectangular table on which was an old manual typewriter. "She wrote here?" I asked. "Yes," Linda answered me. "She particularly loved this window seat area at the front of the parlor. She could spread her pages out on the seat where she

Margaret Mitchell's Typewriter and Writing Table

could see them, and she particularly liked the light through the beveled windows of the alcove."

In a few minutes, Linda and the rest of our tour group left, and Carol and I had a chance to take a few pictures and just think about this place.

"I'm fascinated by her hiding the manila envelopes," I began. "And I'm pretty sure I don't buy the explanation that Mitchell was worried about offending the local residents of Atlanta by writing about the War Between the States. Georgians have always embraced the war. Their state flag, through several permutations, has always been based on one of the flags of the Confederacy. And I don't quite buy her shyness, either," I added.

"Then what would explain the hidden envelopes?" Carol asked.

"Maybe she felt she had discovered something, something about the South, that she knew wouldn't sit well with Southerners—and perhaps not with anyone at all."

"Well, if she was concerned about that, she needn't have been," Carol responded. "Both her book, and then, of course, the movie three years later, have been extraordinarily loved, embraced by audiences from both the North and South."

"Yes," I agreed. "The movie certainly fanned the flame of the book's popularity. But not without making some noteworthy changes."

"Wasn't the movie awfully faithful to the book?" Carol replied. "Much more so than many other movies based on books I know?"

"Yes, it was," I admitted readily. "But it also altered the book into something distinctly different from Mitchell's vision. I think I can illustrate this. First let's look at the opening of the movie where the title of the film is announced to the audience. Then, let's find the moment in the novel where Mitchell first identifies the title of her book for her readers.

"The difference between the two is significant, I think.

"In the film, we first see images of the landscape of Tara, over which moves a text describing the story to come:

> There was a land of
> Cavaliers and Cotton fields
> called the old South...
> Here in this pretty world,
> Gallantry took its last bow...
> Here was the last ever
> to be seen of Knights and their
> Ladies Fair, of Master and of
> Slave.
> Look for it only in books,
> for it is no more than a dream remembered,
> A Civilization gone with the wind...

"Sound familiar?" I asked Carol.

"Of course," she replied. "But I don't recall seeing these words in the book. Mitchell didn't write that, did she?"

"No," I answered her. And then Carol continued, "It sounds more like something Ashley Wilkes would say."

"Exactly," I replied. "And now look at the spot *in the novel* where Mitchell finally introduces the title of her book:

> ...the small cloud which appeared in the northwest four months ago had blown up into a mighty storm and then into a screaming tornado, sweeping away her world,

whirling her out of her sheltered life, and dropping her down into this still, haunted desolation. Was Tara still standing? Or was Tara also gone with the wind which had swept through Georgia? She laid the whip on the tired horse's back and tried to urge him on while the waggling wheels rocked them drunkenly from side to side. (550)

"What did you hear in this passage?" I asked Carol, almost knowing what she was going to say.

"Destruction, loss, fear, weariness, unsteadiness," she answered me, quietly.

"So do I," I added. "And, I'm beginning to believe, that this may explain the hidden envelopes. I think that Mitchell understood, had understood from her childhood, that the South was always ready to talk about the war, about the heroic sacrifices, the gallant bravery, the tenacious dedication of their armies and generals. But not about what she had finally seen for herself–here in this 'Dump' in downtown Atlanta."

"Which was?" Carol asked me.

I could only go back to the very beginning, to that great opening sentence which is so easy to overlook: "That 'Scarlett O'Hara was not beautiful...' " I answered her, and then added "and neither was Rhett Butler, Ashley Wilkes, nor the antebellum South. They all may have had–perhaps even *did* have–a kind of 'charm,' particularly in retrospect, but they each lacked true beauty. I think that that revelation may explain the hidden envelopes."

Suddenly, I added, "And perhaps too it may explain that moment of regret Linda talked about, when Mitchell telegraphed Harold Latham on his train back to New York, urging him to return the manuscript to her. Of course, he didn't. He was already hooked by her extraordinary writing and her vivid characters. But what, Mitchell must have asked herself, might happen if her novel ever appeared in print? What might Southern readers think of her as she revealed that the South's beloved and still venerated "Lost Cause" "was not beautiful"?

Carol's eyes lit up. "And then," she added energetically, "came David O. Selznick."

I could see we were beginning to draw similar conclusions. "Yes," I began, "Selznick made a movie that not only contained the charm Mitchell had identified from the very beginning of her book, but made it beautiful as well. Choosing Vivian Leigh and Clark Gable to play Scarlett and Rhett, visualizing Tara and Twelve Oaks as mansions far exceeding anything that was ever built in Clayton County, Georgia, the film cast the same spell over audiences that the 'glamor' and 'symmetry' of the 'old times' of the South had cast over Ashley.

Movie watchers fell in love with the beauty, the splendor, and the romance of a story that may well have been written with the express intent of dispelling those very illusions.

Fitzgerald Plantation: Margaret Mitchell's Inspiration for Tara

"And that also explains Selznick's omission of two of the novel's important characters: Will and Archie. They're very different people, of course. Will, the poor Cracker Confederate veteran who drifts in to Tara after the war and manages to turn it into a moderately profitable working farm. Archie, the murderer and ex-convict who only gained his freedom by joining the Confederate Army and who has come to stay and help out at the Wilkes's new home in Atlanta. Yet as different as these two characters are, they share one quality of vital importance: each of them is completely impervious to charm. Both men are clear-eyed realists without a trace of sentimentality.

"At Tara, it is Will, not Mammy, who prevents Scarlett's intrusion into Ashley's homecoming embrace with Melanie. Melanie is, after all, Ashley's wife, Will reasons, caring nothing for what Scarlett may or may not be feeling. After Scarlett leaves Tara to pursue her fortune-hunting tactics in Atlanta, Will marries Suellen, establishing his legitimate claim to the land, and runs Tara on a realistic regimen of common sense and hard work. No dreams, no illusions. Just the new way of life in the South after the war.

"And back in Atlanta, when Scarlett hires convicts to work in her mill, Archie summarily refuses to drive her buggy and provide her protection, even though Melanie had asked him to do so. Nothing Scarlett can say or finagle makes any impression on him.

"Selznick didn't want to sully his cinematic dream with such unromantic characters, so he simply banished them from the film. Neither Will nor Archie fit the myth he was trying to create."

Yet here Carol and I stood in the small room where Margaret Mitchell *had* dared to look straight into the mythology that had surrounded her from her youth. *Had* dared to paint her heroine as a deceiving, avaricious manipulator, deluded by the charm of an image of a man of her own creation. *Had* dared to make her hero a self-serving war profiteer and alcoholic womanizer caught by the charm of an impossible dream. *Had* dared to see through the self-deceived lassitude of the Old South and of those unfortunates bewitched by a vision of a life that had never truly existed. *Had* dared, in sum, to see and accept the truth that lay behind it all.

Like "The Dump" in which she lived, this truth was unassuming. Basic. Utilitarian. The city just outside her window was an unimpressive collection of storefronts and places of commerce. None of it was beautiful. Nothing here even hinted of glamor. But it all was real. And in this room Mitchell wrote a great novel about flawed characters and a moment of history that "was not beautiful." A novel that also identified, with uncompromising clarity, the devastatingly high price of charm.

12

Robert Frost

"Something there is..."

Robert Frost's Farm in Derry, New Hampshire

Robert Frost's Pasture: "You come, too."

If ever someone would seem to be justified in claiming himself to be the personification of a region, it would appear to be Robert Frost. From head to foot he was a New England man, plain spoken, gnarled, and stubbornly enduring. He was as undeniably attached to the land as the boulders that shoulder their way up through the tough and unforgiving fields of the farms of New Hampshire and Vermont where he lived for over half a century. Yet the whole truth about Frost is more complicated.

He was born in California, not near the family home in Massachusetts. In later years he would come to prefer withdrawing to his estate in South Miami, Florida, rather than struggling through the harsh and bitter New England winters. His first real literary success had come in England, not the United States. Though he was a staunch Northeastern Yankee, he bore a Confederate general's name (Robert Lee Frost). He was a lifelong Democrat whose roots dug deep into staunchly Republican soil (he called it "infiltrating"). This poet who wrote so straightforwardly was awash in subtle contradictions and complexities. He was beloved as one of our greatest literary figures, but even some of his best known and most widely quoted works have been often misunderstood and misinterpreted by his readers.

As an example of this, consider his famous poem, "The Road Not Taken."

Two roads diverged in a yellow wood,
And sorry I could not travel both
And be one traveler, long I stood
And looked down one as far as I could
To where it bent in the undergrowth;

Then took the other, as just as fair,
And having perhaps the better claim,
Because it was grassy and wanted wear;
Though as for that the passing there
Had worn them really about the same,

And both that morning equally lay
In leaves no step had trodden black.
Oh, I kept the first for another day!
Yet knowing how way leads on to way,
I doubted if I should ever come back.

I shall be telling this with a sigh
Somewhere ages and ages hence:
Two roads diverged in a wood, and I--
I took the one less traveled by,
And that has made all the difference.

Almost from its first appearance in print, this wonderful poem has been interpreted to be an account of the moment in Frost's life when he finally made up his mind to dedicate his life to writing poetry, the less frequented path. By doing so, of course, he was daring to follow his own literary destiny rather than being content simply to accept his family's or his society's expectations of him.

Frost had indeed decided to do precisely this. As soon as his first verses had appeared in print, he had dedicated himself to practicing the art of poetry. But the myriad speakers who have used this poem to urge generations of high school and college graduates to dare to take the road "less traveled by" encounter something of a problem. Not with their advice necessarily, but with the fact that the poem they are citing is actually addressing a distinctly different subject.

Its title, "The Road <u>not</u> Taken," announces the poem's main interest. Its speaker's musings are not concerned with "The Road Taken" nor "The Road I Took" nor even "How to Choose the Best Road To Take." Frost is actually recording a somewhat melancholy account of the doubts and questions that can arise whenever a person takes time to reflect upon his past and on the choices he decided <u>not</u> to make, together with the possible outcomes of those choices, choices now irretrievably lost. Finally, Frost even acknowledges the fact that we sometimes deceive ourselves intentionally in order to lay the ghost of such ruminations.

Readers frequently miss all this, I believe, because it is always more appealing to accept a simple affirmation than it is to confront a complicated and perhaps even unanswerable question. We love happy endings and rejoice in feeling that a difficult life choice has been made correctly. But this poem actually offers no such assurance. It falls into three specific sections, each deserving careful consideration: 1) The past and its dilemma, 2) The honest truth, and 3) The present moment and the lies we tell ourselves.

1) The past and its dilemma

We are first told that at some time in the past the poet had come upon a place in the forest where "Two roads diverged..." He is no longer experiencing this moment but is remembering it. And as he does so he identifies clearly the dilemma it posed, a dilemma that has given rise to his poetic reflections.

Being one person, he cannot travel down both paths simultaneously. Furthermore, traveling down either road will undoubtedly lead him farther and farther away from the road he did not choose. He probably will never have the opportunity to return to the original divergence. And because of this he will never see where the second road might have led him. The dilemma he faces is the need to choose only one of the two roads before him.

2) The honest truth

It was a difficult decision to make. He looked down one path as far as he could see. Then, for no stated reason, he took the other. He tries to assure himself that he had just cause for choosing as he had done ("having perhaps the better claim"). Yet that word "perhaps" suggests that he might only be consoling himself for the moment. In fact, he admits that both paths were essentially "the same," and that neither road was more or less traveled than the other. ("...as for that the passing there/ Had worn them really about the same,/ And both that morning equally lay/ In leaves no step had trodden black.") Both choices, he recalls, were equally appealing, equally beautiful.

3) The present moment and the lies we tell ourselves

And now we arrive at the poet's present, the moment when he is writing this poem and contemplating that at some future date he will be recalling his woodland choice somewhat wistfully ("with a sigh"). If the poem had simply been an account of his success, of his brave decision to follow his dream rather than abandoning his bliss to take a safer road, why would such a remembrance be made "with a sigh"? But then again, Frost is writing about the road "not" taken, acknowledging both its existence and its significance.

Choosing the one road over the other has, after all, "made all the difference." Yet Frost has elected not to specify exactly which of his own life decisions he is recalling here, employing the metaphor of the two diverging woodland roads. This is his own secret, and finally he decides simply not to linger on the memory. He settles for a lie which lays his disquieting questioning to rest: "I took the one less traveled by."

But we know that in fact he had not done so. The earlier verses of the poem admit that each path had lain "equally" appealing and beautiful. Ultimately, however, Frost has to move on past his earlier decision. The unchosen road is unrecoverable, and so it must be dismissed from thought, even if only by a convenient untruth. Frost's willingness to record the complicated thought process of doing so is a large part of the greatness of his poem. He was never interested in simple aphorisms. He thought too much--and too deeply--for that.

On a day in late August of 2016, Carol and I pulled off New Hampshire's Route 28 into the parking lot of Derry Farm, the spot where Robert Frost had lived longer than in any other single location. Our visit to this place would make us feel as if we had walked directly into his poetry.

This farmhouse had been both a gift to, and a challenge set for, the young Robert Frost. His paternal grandfather, William, had almost despaired of his grandson ever making anything worthwhile of himself. A jack of all trades and master of none, for several years Robert Frost had moved from job to job, residence to residence, and into and out of college with neither a marketable degree to show for his efforts nor any perceptible financial progress resulting from his labors. He had married Elinor White in December of 1895 and had fathered two children with her. But the elder, a son named Elliot, died in July of 1900, and the loss of this child had left the young father in a state of serious depression. Yet even at this moment of great need, no profession seemed to catch fire with Robert. He wrote poetry, of course, but William had serious and justifiable doubts about whether or not that "occupation" would ever become successful enough to pay the bills.

Finally, later in 1900 and at Elinor's urging, William purchased a farm near Derry, New Hampshire. Locally it was known as Magoon Place, having been named after an earlier resident. This property William gave to his grandson Robert–with one key condition. The farm and its acreage would be his only after he had lived there and worked it for ten years. If Robert failed to meet this requirement, he would own nothing. Perhaps, William hoped, if his grandson could only be forced to remain stationary for a while, he might gain a clearer sense of direction and purpose in his life.

Robert and his wife accepted this generous, though conditional, offer. They would reside here until they had come into full possession of the property. During their stay, a period in which Frost would later write that all he possessed was "time and seclusion," Elinor would give birth to four more children, and Robert would write what would ultimately become more than two books worth of poetry, poems that would make the reputation and name of Robert Frost internationally famous. Though his grandfather died in 1901 and thus had not lived long enough to see it, his investment in his grandson had borne substantial fruit. Here at Derry Farm, Robert Frost had indeed finally found his life's calling.

The day of Carol's and my visit was pleasantly warm with a clear blue sky overhead punctuated with fluffy white clouds. We exited our rental car and followed a pathway from the parking lot around a large barn which was located behind the farmhouse. Here, we were informed, was where all visitors bought tickets and where our tour of the house would begin.

We were greeted by a friendly gentleman I'll call Jeff who was happy to sell us tickets, but after doing so, he informed us that our tour wouldn't start for another twenty or thirty minutes.

"You can see a video about the Frosts and Derry Farm," he offered us as a way of passing the time.

I mentioned to him that I was writing a book about places where some of our greatest writers had lived and written. His face lit up with a wry and knowing smile, and he added, "OR, you could take a walk around the pasture and into the woods where Frost liked to take his daily rambles. He loved that path so much, he would even clear it in snowy weather, so both he and his family could enjoy the woods year round."

I couldn't help recalling Robert Frost's similar invitation to his readers in his early poem, "The Pasture": "I'm going out to clear the pasture spring...You come too."

"We'll take the walk," I told Jeff, and he nodded rather knowingly it seemed. "I thought you would. Just stay toward the edge of the pasture, and you'll see wooden signs that will show you the way to the path through the forest." He stopped for a moment, then added, "I think you'll find it quite wonderful, and, if needs be, we'll hold the tour for you a couple of minutes."

We checked our watches and then made our way back past the gravel parking lot and into the pasture at the back of the property. It would cast an almost magical effect on us as several of Frost's poems seemed to spring out of the very earth.

We were walking where Robert Frost had walked and worked. Here he had turned the grass and had come upon the tuft of flowers about which he was to write so eloquently. Fringing the field, there were trees, the latest generation of those which, over a century ago, Frost had implored to drop as slowly as possible their leaves now "ripened to the fall" so as to lengthen the October autumn.

And here on the left very near the edge of the pasture was the mending wall that had given rise to one of his most famous poems. His lucid description of the annual event of rebuilding this rough line of demarcation between properties coursed through my mind as we walked by the very place that had inspired the poem:

> *I let my neighbor know beyond the hill;*
> *And on a day we meet to walk the line*
> *And set the wall between us once again.*
> *We keep the wall between us as we go.*
> *To each the boulders that have fallen to each.*
> *And some are loaves and some so nearly balls*
> *We have to use a spell to make them balance:*
> *"Stay where you are until our backs are turned!"*

After a few minutes we reached the end of the pasture and saw a small boulder which clearly marked the spot where a path led into the woods. As we entered this path it immediately diverged, forcing us to choose which way to travel. But these paths were not "roads," so we assumed that the inspiration for "The Road Not Taken" lay elsewhere.

We turned to the right so as to circumnavigate the pasture in the woods and thus ultimately to be able to make our way back toward the house.

It was a heavenly, light-dappled walk, though we had to mind our steps as occasionally a fallen tree trunk or a webbing of roots made the way uneven under foot. A lovely wooden bridge spanned a small stream in the forest, the "west running brook" that Elinor had so loved that she had wished her final resting place to lie near it. By the time of her death in 1937, however, the land had passed out of Frost's hands and the farm had fallen into disrepair and had been "repurposed," as we like to say in the 21st century, into the site of an automobile graveyard. It would ultimately take years of concentrated efforts by Frost, his good friend, John Pillsbury, and Frost's eldest daughter, Lesley, to repurchase the property and bring it back to the condition it had been in at the time of the family's residence there.

Carol and I found an opening where we could easily reenter the pasture and make our way back up to the farmhouse. Our tour of the home was waiting to begin.

Our docent was a pleasant young woman I will name Peggy. She began her commentary in a small room that connected the barn to the house, a room whose chief purpose was obvious to anyone over forty years old.

"It's important to remember," she began, "that this farm had neither electricity nor plumbing at the time the Frost family lived here. That bench over there," she pointed to a small horizontal board with two holes cut in it, "was the only bathroom at the farm." The youngest members of our group were particularly impressed with this piece of information.

"That woodpile," and now Peggy gestured toward a small stack of logs, "is a testament to one of Frost's three favorite tasks. He loved chopping wood to feed the stoves that kept the house warm." There was also an old threshing instrument hanging on the wall, and Peggy now called our attention to it.

"He also loved to scythe wheat, though that may have been more for the sound than anything else. There are numerous places in his poems where he refers to the distinctive whooshing sound the scythe makes as it cuts." She paused a moment before continuing.

"Of course, Robert Frost's third favorite task here at the farm was writing poetry, and now we'll get to see his favorite place to write." And with this comment she invited us all to follow her into the house proper.

Peggy had been informed of my project of writing about authors' homes, and she looked directly at me as we all filed into the bright and cozy kitchen area. She gathered our group around a plain brown rectangular wooden table pushed up against the room's south wall and positioned between two exterior windows. There were four chairs, one on each end and two drawn up facing the wall. The table's surface, however, was not set for serving a meal. On one end was an antique typewriter, the top cover of which was swung open and held some manuscript copy. On the remaining surface area of the table sat an oil lamp and a small vase of flowers.

"It was here at this kitchen table that Frost particularly loved to write," Peggy observed. "For instance, he wrote 'Tree at My Window' while he sat here, looking directly out at that tree there." I bent down to approximate the view Frost must have had, and I think Peggy saw my quizzical expression, as the tree visible from the angle of the chair was still quite a sapling. "Oh, the original tree was lost, but we have planted another right where the first tree stood." Peggy then turned our attention to an old telephone box hung on the west wall of the kitchen.

"The one piece of technology that the farm had was this telephone. It was a party line shared with eight other farm families, and it actually had a profound effect on Frost's poetry. He enjoyed listening in on the conversations that went on between his neighbors and their callers, and this helped him immensely in learning the peculiar phrases and speech patterns of the local population. Remember, Robert Frost was a Californian by birth, so the distinct dialect of New England was not native to him. He had to learn it, and this shared telephone line was his primary teacher."

As Peggy spoke, I found myself reviewing several of Frost's great "conversational" poems which had captured so vividly the language and the unspoken nuances of men and women as they both revealed and attempted to conceal their deepest thoughts and apprehensions. But now our guide was moving on to other matters.

"Robert Frost was never much of a success as a farmer. His grandfather died before the family had lived here a full nine months, and he left his grandson an annuity which provided the family with $800.00 a year, more than enough for them to sustain themselves without having to make the farm profitable. Nevertheless, Frost hired a friend to work the land for him, a man named Carl Burrell, who brought his grandfather, Jonathan Eastman, along with him to help him with such duties as the old man was capable of managing. It was Eastman," Peggy continued, "who died while still here and whose death inspired Frost's great poem, 'The Death of the Hired Man.'"

Moving our group into the next room, a dining room/parlor combination, Peggy informed us that this space had been used to home-school the Frost children. "There was a floor to ceiling bookcase on one wall," she assured us, though there was no vestige of it in evidence anywhere in the room. Peggy also told us about some of the Frosts' unusual child rearing decisions (e.g., There were no assigned beds for the children; they were allowed to sleep wherever they chose to do so, depending on which of their siblings was currently in their good graces). And now Peggy led us to a stairway in the parlor where we were invited to proceed up to the second floor to see the Frosts' master bedroom.

"Elinor had told her husband that her great wish was to wake up with roses every morning," Peggy began as our group gathered in this upstairs bedroom. "So Robert complied by wallpapering the room with a rose patterned design. This current wallpaper was chosen by the Frosts' eldest daughter, Lesley, at the time of the remodeling of the farmhouse, returning it to its earlier appearance." It was a lovely story, and, with the early afternoon sun pouring in through its windows, it was a rather delightful note on which to move toward the end our tour. Peggy briefly showed us the very rudimentary upstairs rooms reserved for Burrell and his grandfather, and then we moved downstairs and back to the barn area where our visit to the farmhouse had begun.

Carol and I decided to see the introductory film, and we enjoyed the images of Frost and various moments of the home's rather colorful history. It was also wonderful to hear Lesley Frost assure us that "The Pasture" had been the first poem her father had written here. In all, Frost's first two books of published poetry, *A Boy's Will* and *North of Boston,* had been largely composed during this period of "time and seclusion," but the imagery of Derry Farm would resonate throughout much of the poetry he would produce for the remainder of his life.

We wandered around the barn a while to view the exhibits there about Frost's life, and then Jeff called me over to the desk behind which he was seated.

"What about this place did you like best?" he asked me.

"I think the walk around the pasture. And the mending wall, particularly. I could really feel the poem coming alive as I stood before it. 'Something there is that doesn't love a wall.' "

Jeff laughed knowingly, and then he posed another question. "And do you know what that 'something' is in truth?"

"You mean, just what is it that, quoting again from the poem, 'sends the frozen groundswell under it, and spills the upper boulders in the sun' ?" I replied.

"Yes," Jeff answered me. "What do you think is the force that causes that damage to those stone walls?"

"Well," I offered, somewhat amusedly, "the poet suggests 'elves' at one point."

"True," Jeff answered, "but there is an actual natural force that pushes the rocks out of position and ultimately creates gaps and spaces in the piled stone property boundary fences."

Jeff had really caught my interest now. "Just what is it?" I asked him.

He smiled, nodded his head briefly, and gave me a one word response. "Frost," he said.

It was a perfect answer. A perfect coda to our visit here. As Carol and I returned to our car and slowly backed out of our parking space, I recounted to her this final conversation with Jeff. She smiled as I finished.

"Frost. Of course. It had to be." And then she added, "It's perfect."

We were both quietly thoughtful as I pulled our rental car back out onto Highway 28 which ran surprisingly close to the front of the farm. Once again, Carol and I were traveling together on country roads. We had about fifty miles left to drive today, all on two lane highways. And although there were friends who were waiting to greet us, Robert Frost was still occupying our thoughts. "Time and seclusion," I found myself saying aloud. "What better gift could anyone give a poet?" Carol smiled and nodded. For us on this afternoon, though, it was "miles to go before" we would sleep. But at least we were bringing Frost along with us. With each passing mile we were journeying deeper and deeper into "New Hampshire." And that of course was leading us farther and farther "North of Boston."

Locations Visited

(Note: Many locations contain more than one home, a museum, and/or an additional site nearby. We recommend you call ahead for hours, special events, closures, etc.)

Washington Irving (1783-1859)

Washington Irving's Sunnyside (914) 366-6900
3 W Sunnyside Lane
Irvington NY 10533

Henry Wadsworth Longfellow (1807-1882)

The Wadsworth-Longfellow House (207) 774-1822
489 Congress Street
Portland ME 041901

Longfellow House/Washington's Headquarters (617) 876-4491
105 Brattle Street
Cambridge MA 02138

The Wayside Inn (978) 443-1776
72 Wayside Inn Road
Sudbury MA 01776

Ralph Waldo Emerson (1803-1882)

The Home of Ralph Waldo Emerson ("Bush") (978) 369-2236
28 Cambridge Turnpike at Lexington Rd
Concord MA 01742

The Old Manse (978) 369-3909
269 Monument Street
Concord MA 01742-1837

Marat House (Privately owned)
Bridge and St. George Street in St. Augustine, FL

Henry David Thoreau (1817-1862)

Henry David Thoreau's Birthplace
341 Virginia Road
Concord MA 01742
Mailing address: PO Box 454
Concord MA 01742

Concord's Colonial Inn (978) 369-9200
48 Monument Square
Concord MA 01742

Walden Pond State Reservation (978) 369-3254
915 Walden Street
Concord MA 01742

Bronson (1799-1888) and Louisa May Alcott (1832-1888)

Fruitlands Museum (978) 456-3924
102 Prospect Hill Road
Harvard MA 01451

Louisa May Alcott's Orchard House (978) 369-4118
399 Lexington Road
Concord MA 01742

The Wayside: Home of Authors (978) 318-7825
455 Lexington Road
Concord MA 01742

Nathaniel Hawthorne (1804-1864)

The House of the Seven Gables (978) 744-0991
115 Derby Street
Salem MA 01970

Salem Maritime: The Custom House (978) 740-1650
160 Derby Street
Salem MA 01970

The Old Manse (978) 369-3909
269 Monument Street
Concord MA 01742-1837

The Wayside: Home of Authors (978) 318-7825
455 Lexington Road
Concord MA 01742

Emily Dickinson (1830-1886)

The Homestead and Evergreens (413) 542-8161
280 Main Street
Amherst MA 01002

Harriet Beecher Stowe (1811-1896)

Harriet Beecher Stowe House (513) 751-0651
2950 Gilbert Avenue
Cincinnati OH 45206

The Harriet Beecher Stowe House (207) 725-3000
or (207) 725-3253
63 Federal Street
Brunswick ME 04011

Harriet Beecher Stowe Center (860) 522-9258
77 Forest Street
Hartford CT 06105

Mark Twain (1835-1910)

Mark Twain Birthplace State Historic Site (573) 565-3449
37352 Shrine Road
Florida MO 65283-2127

The Mark Twain Boyhood Home and Museum (573) 221-9010
120 North Main Street
Hannibal MO 63401

The Mark Twain House and Museum (860) 247-0998
351 Farmington Avenue
Hartford CT 06105

Mark Twain's Study (607) 735-1800
(located on the campus of Elmira College)
One Park Place
Elmira NY 14901

(Important Note: The site of John Quarles's farm located near Florida, Missouri, as well as the site of Quarry Farm, near Elmira, New York, are not open to the public. Both are privately owned.)

Ernest Hemingway (1898-1961)

The Ernest Hemingway Home and Museum (305) 294-1136
907 Whitehead Street
Key West FL 33040

Margaret Mitchell (1900-1949)

Margaret Mitchell House and Museum (404) 249-7015
979 Crescent Avenue NE
Atlanta GA 30309

Stately Oaks Plantation (770) 473-0197
100 Carriage Lane at Jodeco Road
Jonesboro GA 30236-8114

Road to Tara Museum (770) 478-4800
104 N Main Street
Jonesboro GA 30236-8315

Marietta *Gone with the Wind* Museum (770) 479-5576
472 Powder Springs Street
Marietta GA 30064

Robert Frost (1874-1963)

The Robert Frost Farm (603) 432-3091
122 Rockingham Road
Derry NH 03038

A Select Bibliography

1. Abel, Darrel. "Mark Twain." In *American Literature: Masterworks of American Realism*. Woodbury, New York: Barron's Educational Series, 1963.
2. Alcott, A. Bronson. *Concord Days*. Boston: Roberts Brothers, 1872.
3. ------. *Tablets*. Boston: Robert Brothers, 1868.
4. Alcott, Louisa May. *Little Women*. New York: Barnes & Noble Classics, 2004.
5. ------. "Transcendental Wild Oats." In *Bronson Alcott's Fruitlands*. Bedford, MA, Applewood Books, 2004.
6. Bedell, Madelon. *The Alcotts: Biography of a Family*. New York: Clarkson N. Potter, Inc., 1980.
7. Bliss, Donald Tiffany. *Mark Twain's Tale of Today*. North Charleston, SC: CreateSpace, 2012.
8. Brenner, Gerry. "View Points." In *Twentieth Century Interpretations of Walden*. Ed. Richard Rutland. Englewood Cliffs, NJ: Prentice-Hall, 1968.
9. Brown, Ellen, and John Wiley, Jr. *Margaret Mitchell's Gone with the Wind*. Lanham, MD: Taylor Trade Publishing, 2011.
10. Budd, Louis J., ed. *New Essays on Adventures of Huckleberry Finn*. Cambridge: Cambridge University Press, 1985.
11. Burstein, Andrew. *The Original Knickerbocker: The Life of Washington Irving*. New York: Basic Books, 2007.
12. Cheever, Susan. *American Bloomsbury*. New York: Simon & Schuster, 2006.

13. ───────. *Louisa May Alcott*. New York: Simon & Schuster, 2010.

14. Clemens, Clara. *Awake to a Perfect Day*. New York: The Citadel Press, 1956.

15. Cooper, Robert. *Around the World with Mark Twain*. New York: Arcade Publishing, 2000.

16. David, Beverly R., and Ray Sapistein. "Illustrators and Illustrations in Mark Twain's First American Editions." In *Following the Equator and Anti-Imperialist Essays*. Ed. Shelley Fisher Fishkin. New York: Oxford University Press, 1966.

17. Dickinson, Emily. *Poems of Emily Dickinson*. New York: The Limited Editions Club, 1952.

18. Emerson, Ralph Waldo. *Essays*. Boston: Houghton, Mifflin and Company, 1892.

19. ───────. *Nature, Addresses, and Lectures*. Boston: Houghton, Mifflin and Company, 1892.

20. Emerson, Ralph Waldo and Henry David Thoreau. *Nature Walking*. Boston: Beacon Press, 1994.

21. Frost, Robert. *The Collected Poems of Robert Frost*. New York: Henry Holt and Company, 1939.

22. ───────. "View Points." In *Twentieth Century Interpretations of Walden*. Ed. Richard Rutland. Englewood Cliffs, NJ: Prentice-Hall, 1968.

23. Garber, Frederick. *Thoreau's Redemptive Imagination*. New York: New York University Press, 1977.

24. Griffin, Patricia C. "Ralph Waldo Emerson in St. Augustine." In *El Escribano: The St. Augustine Journal of History* Volume 32. St. Augustine, FL: St. Augustine Historical Society, 1995.

25. Gross, Seymour L., ed. *A Scarlet Letter Handbook*. San Francisco: Wadsworth Publishing Company, Inc., 1960.

26. Hawthorne, Nathaniel. *Mosses From an Old Manse*. New York: Modern Library, 2003.

27. -------. *The Scarlet Letter*. New York: The Modern Library, 2000.

28. Hemingway, Ernest. *The Old Man and the Sea*. New York: Charles Scribner's Sons, 1952.

29. -------. *To Have and Have Not*. New York: Scribner, 2003.

30. Howells, William Dean. *My Mark Twain*. Mineola, NY: Dover Publications, Inc., 1997.

31. Irving, Washington. *A History of New York*. New York: G. P. Putnam's Sons, 1889.

32. -------. *Astoria*. New York: G. P. Putnam's Sons, 1889.

33. -------. *The Crayon Miscellany*. New York: G. P. Putnam's Sons, 1865.

34. -------. *The Sketch Book*. New York: G. P. Putnam's Sons, 1890.

35. -------. *Wolfert's Roost*. New York: G. P. Putnam's Sons, 1865.

36. Kaplan, Fred. *The Singular Mark Twain*. New York: Doubleday, 2003.

37. Kaplan, Justin. *Mr. Clemens and Mr. Twain: A Biography*. New York: Simon and Schuster, 1966.

38. Krutch, Joseph Wood. *Henry David Thoreau*. New York: William Sloan Associates, 1948.

39. Longfellow, Henry Wadsworth. *The Poems of Henry Wadsworth Longfellow*. Ed. Louis Untermeyer. New York: The Heritage Press, 1943.

40. Marshall, Megan. *The Peabody Sisters*. Boston: Houghton Mifflin Company, 2006.

41. Matteson, John. *Eden's Outcasts*. New York: W. W. Norton & Company, 2007.

42. Matthiessen, F.O. *American Renaissance*. New York: Oxford University Press, 1941.

43. McFarland, Philip. *Hawthorne in Concord*. New York: Grove Press, 2004.
44. McLendon, James. *Papa: Hemingway in Key West*. Key West, FL: Langley Press, Inc., 1990.
45. Michelson, Bruce. *Printer's Devil*. Berkley, CA: University of California Press, 2006.
46. Mitchell, Margaret. *Gone with the Wind*. New York: Macmillan Publishing Co., 1936.
47. Noble, David W. *The Eternal Adam and the New World Garden*. New York: Grosset Dunlap, 1968.
48. Paine, Albert Bigelow. *Mark Twain: A Biography*. 3 vol. New York: Chelsea House, 1980.
49. Peabody, Elizabeth. *Record of a School*. Bedford, MA: Applewood Books, 2006.
50. Powers, Ron. *Dangerous Water*. Cambridge, MA: Da Capo Press, 1999.
51. -------. *Mark Twain: A Life*. New York: Free Press, 2005.
52. Quirk, Tom. *Mark Twain and Human Nature*. Columbia, MO: University of Missouri Press, 2007.
53. Rasmussen, R. Kent. *Mark Twain A-Z*. New York: Oxford University Press, 1995.
54. Ruland, Richard, ed. *Twentieth Century Interpretations of Walden*. Englewood Cliffs, NJ: Prentice-Hall, 1968.
55. Sayre, Robert F., ed. *New Essays on Walden*. Cambridge: Cambridge University Press, 1992.
56. Schreiner, Samuel A., Jr. *The Concord Quartet*. Hoboken, NJ: John Wiley & Sons, Inc., 2006.
57. Scott, Arthur L. *Mark Twain at Large*. Chicago: Henry Regnery Company, 1969.
58. Shelden, Michael. *Mark Twain: Man in White*. New York: Random House, 2010.

59. Simpson, Claude M., ed. *Twentieth Century Interpretations of Adventures of Huckleberry Finn*. Englewood Cliffs, NJ: Prentice-Hall, Inc., 1968.

60. Spiller, Robert E. *The Cycle of American Literature*. New York: The Free Press, 1955.

61. Stowe, Harriet Beecher. *Palmetto Leaves*. Gainesville: University Press of Florida, 1999.

62. -------. *Uncle Tom's Cabin*. New York: The Modern Library, 2001.

63. Sullivan, Robert. *The Thoreau You Don't Know*. New York: HarperCollins Publishers, 2009.

64. Thoreau, Henry David. *Walden and Civil Disobedience*. New York: W.W. Norton and Company, Inc., 1966.

65. Thorpe, James. *Thoreau's Walden*. San Marino, CA: The Huntington Library, 1977.

66. Twain, Mark. *The Adventures of Huckleberry Finn*. New York: The Modern Library, 2001.

67. -------. *Autobiography of Mark Twain, The*. Ed. Charles Neider. New York: Harper and Row Publishers, 1959.

68. -------. *Following the Equator* (American Artists Edition). New York: Harper and Brothers, 1925.

69. -------. *Life on the Mississippi* (American Artists Edition). New York: Harper and Brothers, 1917.

70. -------. *Mark Twain in Eruption*. Ed. Bernard Devoto. New York: Harper and Brothers Publishers, 1922.

71. -------. *Sketches New and Old* (American Artists Edition). New York: Harper and Brothers, 1917.

72. Ward, Geoffrey C., Dayton Duncan, and Ken Burns. *Mark Twain: An Illustrated Biography*. New York: Alfred A. Knopf, 2001.

73. Wecter, Dixon. *Sam Clemens of Hannibal*. Boston: Houghton Mifflin Co., 1952.

74. Weeks, Robert P., ed. *Hemingway: A Collection of Critical Essays*. Englewood Cliffs, NJ: Prentice-Hall, Inc., 1962.

75. Williams, George, III. *Mark Twain: His Life in Virginia City, Nevada*. Riverside, CA: Tree by the River Publishing, 1985.

76. Willis, Resa. *Mark and Livy*. New York: TV Books, 1992.

77. Wilson, Sullivan. *New England Men of Letters*. New York: Macmillan Publishing Co., Inc., 1972.

78. Zacks, Richard. *Chasing the Last Laugh*. New York: Doubleday, 2016.

[Note: Quotations from Mark Twain's *Following the Equator* come from Harper and Brothers two-volume American Artists edition. The number before the backslash indicates the volume #; the number(s) after the backslash indicate the page(s) cited. The illustrations come from the first American edition published by The American Publishing Company in 1897.]

Afterword

As I draw to a close in writing this book about the "Inspiration Points" of the twelve American authors I have presented here, I find myself full of gratitude. As individual as the experience of writing would appear to be, the fact is that a great number of people have contributed to my insights and conclusions.

I have often observed that when teachers have written books, they frequently thank their students for their support and encouragement. I certainly share this feeling, but I would like to specify precisely what I mean by that gratitude, and to do that, I have to first thank one of my favorite college professors: Ron Burnett.

When I first took a class with him at Principia College, I was struck, day after day, by two things. First, he crafted his sentences and his vocabulary with such precision that I immediately made it a goal to both appreciate and emulate the same care in my own use of language. Second, Ron had an extraordinary interest in actually listening to his students. He invariably made his classes feel as if they were on the very cusp of discovery, that what they were discussing had never been discerned before by anyone else. That they were breaking new ground, even when analyzing works that had been studied by scholars for many years.

I remember asking Ron once about how he helped his classes feel this way, and his answer made an enormous impact on me. "Because it's true," he said simply.

"But how can it be true, Ron?" I asked him. "Surely, you know so much more than your students that their observations, however good, aren't surprising to you."

He paused before continuing. "Clark, I don't think you have understood yet the extraordinary contribution that any student in a class can bring to a discussion." He saw me look inquiringly at him before he spoke again. "A first reading with fresh eyes. You see, when I assign a book to a class, I already think I know its value and its important passages and characters. I have already read it, usually many times before, and I have researched and been taught to recognize where its inspiration lies and what constitutes its significance. But a student, even the most callow freshman who has never read the work before, sees it without any of those points of view. It's amazing to me how a student can find meaning in places in a text where I had never seen it. Not every student every time, of course," he added, "but often enough that it makes me always want to listen and learn."

By the time we were having this conversation, Ron knew that I had decided to pursue teaching as a career. So he added, "Try it, Clark. Try seeing things in texts that your training never prepared you to see. Once you do, you'll never want to teach in any other way."

So when I thank you, the young men and women whom I have had the privilege of teaching over the years, I'm thanking you for the many inspirations and revelations your "first readings with fresh eyes" have brought to me and to our classes together. I've learned to love literature with greater depth and renewed wonder because of your insights and your willingness to forward ideas that came to you as you read. You proved to me repeatedly just how right Ron Burnett's advice had been.

Afterword

To Carol, to whom this book is lovingly and happily dedicated: your patience and tireless efforts as trip planner, editor, encourager, and best friend have made this book possible. You are "the light of my life" and sharing these adventures with you has been a total joy. "What larks!"

And many thanks to some specific individuals who have been wonderful friends and helpful listeners throughout this process. To Jim Evans, my longtime teaching colleague and friend: what a debt I owe to you. You who walked Walden with me in the summer heat and visited so many of the Concord locations. You–and your precious wife Lynne–who rode the catamaran over washboard waves all the way from Fort Myers to Key West (and back again!) so Carol and I could visit the Hemingway house–and then drove around in a rental electric car for an hour while we visited the home because there were no available parking places nearby. What a friend you are and a great teacher as well. Your friendship means the world to me.

To Henry Sweets, curator and recently retired Executive Director of the Mark Twain Boyhood Home and Museum in Hannibal, Missouri: I am deeply grateful for the many occasions when we toured the properties in Hannibal together, and the hours of conversations we have had as you assisted me in deepening my understanding of Mark Twain.

And then there were the readers of portions of my manuscript on numerous occasions: Jim Evans, again; Hal and Bonnie Hoerner, whose interest in and encouragement of this project has meant so much; Nancy Bourcier, a longtime friend and supporter of my creative endeavors whose watchful eye for detail has been such a help; Bruce Butterfield who was supportive of this project throughout its progress; Duane Christianson and Toni Youngblood, two wonderful friends who were willing to help me see when my focus needed refinement and redirection in my introductory chapter. To all of you, my heartfelt thanks.

To Joanne Root-Knight: Carol and I so appreciated your and Bob's welcome to your lovely home in the heart of literary New England. And to Karen Hunt: thank you for your tour of the fascinating Quarry Farm property and the reconstruction of the farmhouse there.

To the many docents and park employees who spend their lives introducing visitors to the homes and works of these writers: I admire your passion and your dedication. You are essential to the memory of these authors. I hope you see my gratitude for and indebtedness to you all in my descriptions of the locations in your care.

To my children and extended family who always followed my efforts in bringing this book to fruition: my heartfelt thanks for your interest in and encouragement of this project.

And lastly, to my current readers: I'm grateful for your desire to learn more about these great American authors. I hope this account of Carol's and my travels will encourage you to make excursions of your own. Happy voyaging to you all.

About the Author

Clark Beim-Esche earned his undergraduate and graduate degrees from Northwestern University. During his over 40 years of teaching College, Secondary School, and Lifelong Learning classes, Clark has presented courses on American Literature and American History, Fine Arts, and Film. In 2008, he received the Mark Twain Boyhood Home and Museum Creative Teaching Award. Since his retirement in 2010, Clark and his wife Carol have traveled extensively throughout the United States doing research for both his book *Calling on the Presidents: Tales Their Houses Tell* and this current work *Inspiration Points: Where Our Writers Wrote*. A gifted storyteller, Clark has lectured nationally and internationally on such topics as Presidential Homes, The Bill of Rights, The Declaration of Independence, Mark Twain, American Masterpieces, Fine Arts, and Film.

Books and ebooks are available online. To order a book, send a response, or to schedule a book talk for your organization, please go to:

www.clarkbeim-esche.vpweb.com/